Highlights

2
SECOND GRADE
AGES 7-8

Second Grade
Big Fun Workbook

P9-CEJ-254

For information about permission to reproduce selections from this book for
an entire school or school district, please contact permissions@highlights.com.

Published by Highlights Learning • 815 Church Street • Honesdale, Pennsylvania 18431
ISBN: 978-1-68437-158-7
Mfg. 09/2020
Printed in Mattoon, IL, USA
First edition
10 9 8 7 6 5

For assistance in the preparation of this book, the editors would like to thank:
Vanessa Maldonado, MSEd; MS Literacy Ed. K–12; Reading/LA Consultant Cert.; K–5 Literacy Instructional Coach
Kristin Ward, MS Curriculum, Instruction, and Assessment; K–5 Mathematics Instructional Coach
Jump Start Press, Inc.

It's Time for Big Fun!

The pages of this book are filled with hundreds of curriculum-based puzzles and activities to help your child succeed in second grade—in areas such as phonics, parts of speech, vocabulary, reading, writing, addition, subtraction, time and money, shapes, place value, and science and social studies concepts.

How to use this book:

1 Find the right time.
Your second grader may be tired and hungry after school, so you may want to wait to introduce a new activity when she is well fed and rested.

2 Let your child take the lead.
There is no single "right way" to do this book. Let your child select the activities that interest him most and do them at a pace that works for him.

3 Set a good example.
Try sitting down with your child to do some of your own "work" while your child does her activities. This way, you'll be right there to guide her if she needs it.

4 Pour on the praise.
When your child works hard to complete a page, acknowledge his efforts enthusiastically.

5 Encourage cooperation and teamwork.
If you see your child struggling with a concept, offer to work together as a team. Give her clues if you like, but don't provide answers for her.

Contents

Alphabet Maze

Alphabetical Order

Annie's and Zeke's buses take different routes to school. Trace Annie's bus' path by following the uppercase letters in alphabetical order. Trace Zeke's bus' path by following the lowercase letters in alphabetical order.

A to Z Train Station

Find at least one thing in this scene that starts with each letter of the alphabet. Cross off each letter as you find something that begins with that letter.

A
B
C
D
E
F
G
H
I
J
K
L
M
N
O
P
Q
R
S
T
U
V
W
X
Y
Z

Phonics: Beginning Sounds

Missing Letters

Write the missing consonant.

_Cookie

_Kite

_Tiger

_horn

_olcano

_cuarter

_adder

_magnet

_utton

Missing Letters

Write the missing consonant.

whee__

boo__

rocke__

dolphi__

lunchbo__

we__

pi__

ma__

cactu__

Write the missing vowel.

 cr__b

 t__nt

 m__p

 starf__sh

 j__m

 m__g

 zebr__

 p__nny

 rob__t

Animal Beats

Say each animal name in the word bank slowly and count the beats. Write the names with one, two, three, and four syllables in each box. We filled in one of each to get you started.

alligator   armadillo   bear   butterfly   caterpillar

elephant   flamingo   fox   frog   hippopotamus

kangaroo   lion   monkey   octopus   rhinoceros

rooster   salamander   snake   tiger   whale   zebra

1 syllable

fox

2 syllables

monkey

3 syllables

butterfly _____

_____

_____

_____

4 syllables

alligator _____

_____

_____

_____

One animal name is left. It has **5 syllables**. Write the animal name here.

_____

What's That Sound?

Write each word from the word bank in the box with the matching short-vowel sound. Say each word as you write it. We filled in one of each to get you started.

bed   bib   can   cap   ~~crab~~   cub   dog   ~~duck~~
fin   ~~fox~~   ~~hen~~   jet   kit   mop   pen   ~~pig~~   pin
pot   rag   rug   sock   sun   tub   van   web

Short a   crab
_____
_____
_____
_____

Short e   hen
_____
_____
_____
_____

Short *i*

pig

_____

_____

_____

_____

Short *o*

fox

_____

_____

_____

_____

Short *u*

duck

_____

_____

_____

_____

Silent-*e* Machine

Read each short-vowel word aloud. Add a silent *e* to the end. Write and say the new long-vowel word.

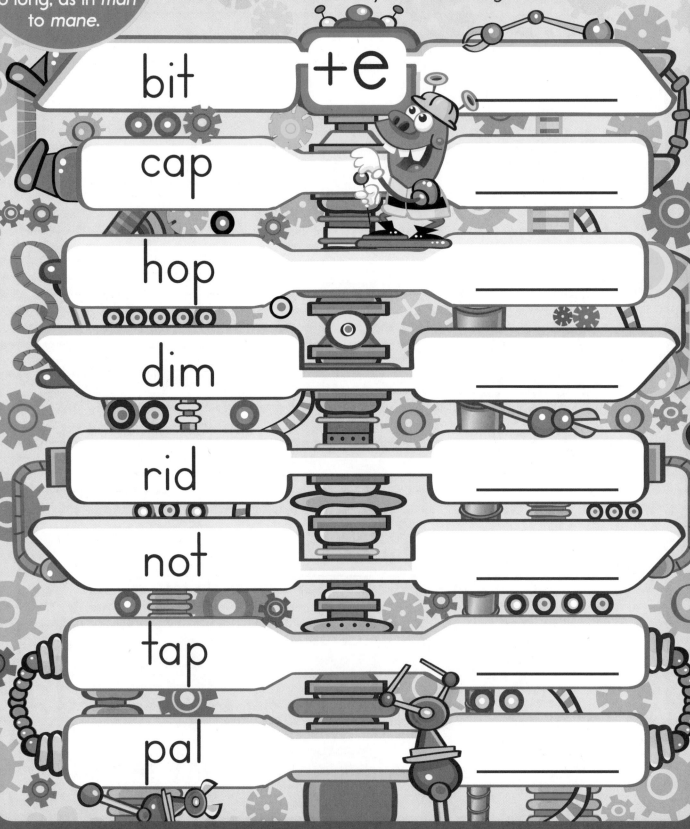

+e

bit _____

cap _____

hop _____

dim _____

rid _____

not _____

tap _____

pal _____

Phonics and Spelling: Silent *e*

Read each long-vowel word aloud. Take away the silent **e**. Write and say the new short-vowel word.

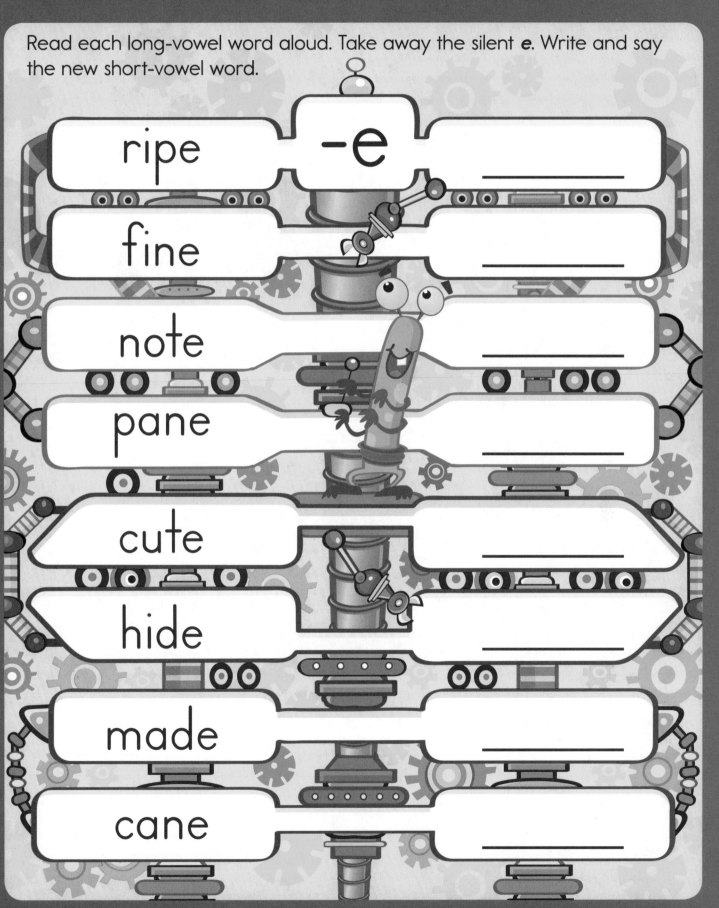

-e

ripe   _____

fine   _____

note   _____

pane   _____

cute   _____

hide   _____

made   _____

cane   _____

Bake Sale

Phonics and Spelling: Long Vowels and Silent *e*

At this sale, you'll find cakes in all sizes and shapes! Find and circle **15** objects whose names include include a long vowel and silent **e** in this Hidden Pictures® puzzle.

vase

cane

kite

lime

dime

plane

rope

dice

tape

flute

pine

rose

globe

frame

skate

Prairie Dog Days

Write long-**a** words from the word bank to complete the stories. Say each word as you write it.

The long **a** sound can be spelled *ai*, as in *rain*; or *ay*, as in *ray*; or *a* on its own, as in *apron*.

acorns	drain	flavor	play
stay	table	today	trail	wait

Ray has big plans for _____.
He wrote some new music he will try to
_____ on his piano. He wants
to _____ inside all day.

· ·

Ada wants to read her new book while she
munches some _____. She has a
cup of tea on the _____ to enjoy
later. She loves the _____ of tea.

· ·

Bailey can't _____ to get to
her den. She stopped the _____
in her tub to draw a hot bath. Which
_____ takes her home?

Trace the trails to help each prairie dog get home.

Meet at the Beach

The long e sound can be spelled *ea*, as in *heat*; *ie*, as in *chief*; or *ee*, as in *sweet*.

Write **ea**, **ie**, or **ee** to complete the words.

I love the b＿＿ch. I m＿＿t my friends there at least once a w＿＿k in the summer. You n＿＿d to be a good swimmer to go in the s＿＿ and always stay within r＿＿ch of a lifeguard.

We like to lie on a big blanket and r＿＿d books. I always bring a p＿＿ce of fruit to share. Today I packed a big, juicy p＿＿ch. My friends bring snacks too, so we have a f＿＿st.

After we ＿＿t, I lie back and enjoy the warm, gentle br＿＿ze. Sometimes I bel＿＿ve it even puts me to sl＿＿p.

What silly things do you see?

21

What did the beach say when the tide came in?

"Long time no sea."

EAT AT JOE'S

49¢

I Like Knights

The long *i* sound can be spelled *igh*, as in *light*; *ie*, as in *pie*; or *i* on its own, as in *iron*.

Help the knight find his way across the castle from **START** to **FINISH**. He can only travel through words with the long *i* sound.

Hello, O!

The long o sound can be spelled *oa*, as in *boat*, or *ow*, as in *low*.

Write the **ow** words from the word bank under the boy tying a bow. Write the **oa** words under the boy holding a boat. Say each word as you write it.

arrow	bowl	coat	glow
loaf	slow	soap	toad	toast	yellow

ow

oa

_____

_____

_____

_____

O at the end of a syllable is always long o.

Circle the names of the musical intruments that begin or end with the long **o** sound. What sound do the others end with?

banjo   cello
harmonica   oboe   piano
piccolo   tuba

Clues to Chew On

Fill in this grid with the long-*u* words listed below. Use the number of letters in each word as a clue to where it might fit. We did one to get you started.

3 Letters
EMU
NEW

4 Letters
BLUE
CHEW
CLUE
GLUE
GREW
SUIT
TRUE

5 Letters
FRUIT
HUMAN
JUICE
MUSIC
THREW

6 Letters
CRUISE

7 Letters
UNICORN
UNIFORM

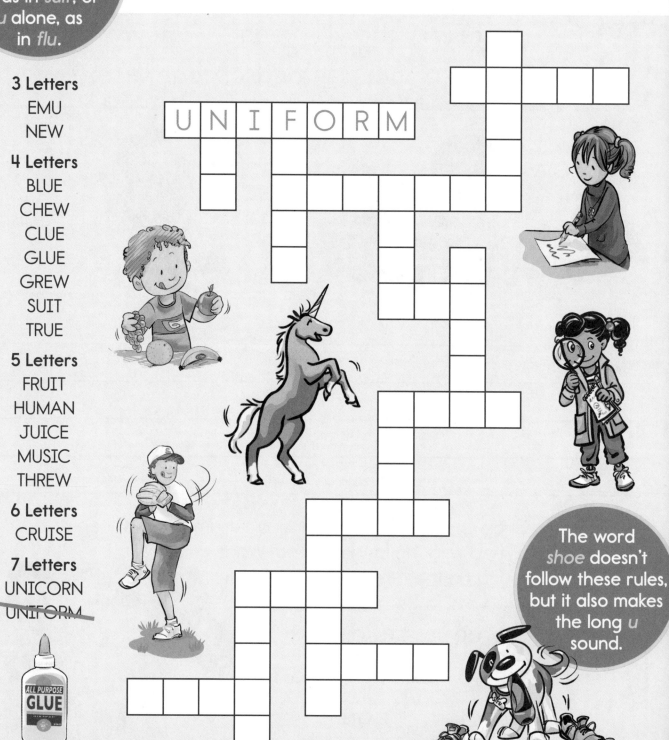

The word *shoe* doesn't follow these rules, but it also makes the long *u* sound.

Mighty Y

At the end of a one-syllable word, *y* often has the long *i* sound, as in *my*. At the end of a two-syllable word, *y* often has the long *e* sound, as in *fuzzy*.

Read the words in the word bank. If the *y* at the end of the word sounds like **long i**, write the word under the spy. If the **y** sounds like **long e**, write the word under the mummy.

city   cry   daisy   dry   fly   fry
happy   silly   sky   sunny   tiny   try

_____   _____

_____   _____

_____   _____

_____   _____

Butterfly has **3** syllables.
What sound does the **y** make?

Snail Mail

Phonics and Spelling: Long Vowel Sounds

Find and circle **15** objects whose names include long vowel combinations in this Hidden Pictures® puzzle.

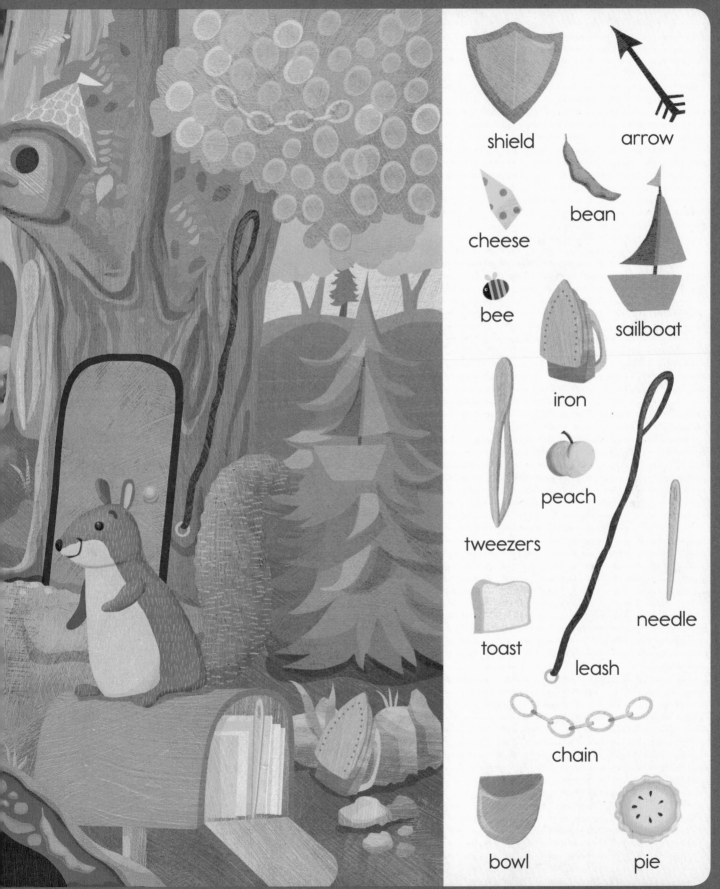

shield

arrow

bean

cheese

sailboat

bee

iron

peach

tweezers

needle

toast

leash

chain

bowl

pie

Farm Party

Phonics and Spelling: *R*-Controlled Vowels

Can you find a star, a ladder, a bird, a fork, and a turkey? What else do you see that is spelled with *ar, er, ir, or,* or *ur*? What silly things do you see?

When the letter *r* comes after a vowel, it changes the vowel sound.

Which Pair to Wear?

The *air* sound can be spelled *air*, as in *chair*; *are*, as in *share*; or *ear*, as in *wear*.

A **homophone** is word that is pronounced like another word but has a different spelling. Circle the homophone that completes each sentence.

I can't find a (pear/pair) of mittens to match!

Count the steps as you climb the (stairs/stares).

I rode the carousel at the (fair/fare).

The sand is soft and warm on my (bear/bare) feet.

I wear my (hair/hare) in a ponytail when I play soccer.

How many pairs of mittens can you find? Which mittens don't have a match?

Near the Pier

The *ear* sound can be spelled *ear*, as in *dear*; *eer*, as in *cheer*; *ere*, as in *here*; *eir*, as in *weird*; or *ier*, as in *pier*.

Write the words from the word bank to complete the story. Say each word as you write it.

clear   deer   fear   here   near   steer   weird

The water is _____ as we set out. Greer tries to _____ as we float down the river. We spot a _____ and her doe on the bank. We see a _____ rock that looks like monster. "Have no _____," says Greer. "We're _____ our next stop." A few minutes later, she says, "We're _____!"

Help the kids find their way to the pier.

What I Saw at Dawn

Write the words from the word bank to complete the poem. Say each word as you write it.

The *aw* sound can be spelled *aw*, as in *straw*, or *au*, as in *launch*.

because	claws	dawn
lawn	pause	yawn

This morning at _____
    I awoke with a _____,
    and saw something land on our front
    _____.

The sight made me _____,
    and that is _____
    it had feathers, large wings, a sharp
    beak . . . and _____!

What did the boy see? Connect the dots to find out.

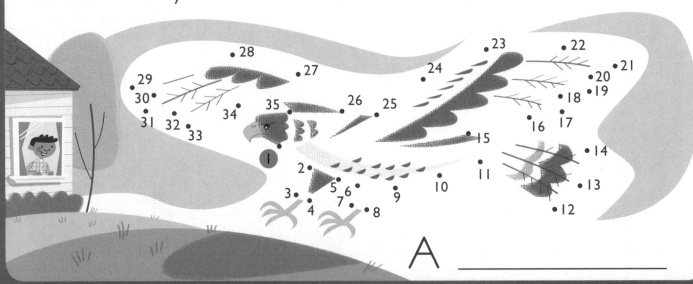

A _____

Let's All Walk

The *all* sound can be spelled *al*, as in *chalk* or *all*, as in *tall*.

Write the words from the word bank to complete the story. Say each word as you write it.

> ball call fall malt salt small talk walk wall

The sun is shining as we _____ to the beach. We can smell the _____ in the air. We build a sandcastle with a _____ around it. I find a _____ seashell to add.

"Don't let it _____!" shouts Layla as someone throws a _____ near us.

We _____ about what to do next. The _____ of seagulls searching for lunch makes us hungry.

"Let's get an ice-cream _____!" I say.

How many beach balls can you spot?

Wow!

Dipthongs are 2 vowels that go together to make a brand-new sound.

Write **oi** or **oy** to complete the words.

I love my flying pig t＿＿.

I saved up my c＿＿ns to buy it.

When you hug the pig, it says "＿＿nk!"

Sometimes the n＿＿se makes me laugh.

My pig brings me great j＿＿.

Write the **ou** and **ow** words from the word bank to complete the story. Say each word as you write it.

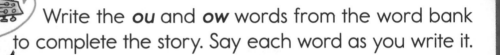

count   crowd   house   howl
loud   mouse   now   sound   wow

What's that ＿＿＿＿＿＿＿＿? It's our new band!

We can be as quiet as a ＿＿＿＿＿＿ or as

＿＿＿＿＿ as a lion. Sometimes my dog will

＿＿＿＿＿ when we sing. We ＿＿＿＿＿ the

beats to the music so we can play together.

Someday, we'll ＿＿＿＿＿ a huge ＿＿＿＿＿. But

for ＿＿＿＿＿, we just play inside my ＿＿＿＿＿.

Cool at the Pool

Double o makes 2 different sounds, as in *book* or as in *spoon*.

Can you find a cookie and a poodle in this silly scene?
What else do you see that is spelled with a **double o**?
Which items make the same sound as the **oo** in *cookie*?
Which items make the same sound as the **oo** in *poodle*?

What does a cookie say when it's excited?

"Chip, chip, hooray!"

Chef Steve's Blends

A blend is when each letter in a group of consonants makes its own sound, like *bl* in *blue*. A digraph is when 2 consonants make a new sound together, like *sh* in *show*.

cl gr wh
br th sh
tr cr
ch dr
st
fl
sl sn sp
bl

Chef Steve cooks spinach but not kale.
He'll serve shakes but not juice,
Blueberries but not apples,
And flan, but never mousse.
Chef Steve makes a great grilled cheese
And a spicy chicken stew,
But he'd never bake a turkey dinner.
He knows why—do you?

Add Chef Steve's consonant blends and digraphs to each word ending.
Can you make 5 words with each? We did one to get you started.

bl	br	ch	cl	cr	dr	fl	gr
sh	sl	sn	sp	st	th	tr	wh

f l y   _ _ y | _ _ ip   _ _ ip | _ _ at   _ _ at
_ _ y   _ _ y | _ _ ip   _ _ ip | _ _ at   _ _ at
_ _ y | _ _ ip | _ _ at

_ _ in   _ _ in | _ _ ab   _ _ ab | _ _ ade   _ _ ade
_ _ in   _ _ in | _ _ ab   _ _ ab | _ _ ade   _ _ ade
_ _ in | _ _ ab | _ _ ade

_ _ im   _ _ im | _ _ ink   _ _ ink | _ _ are   _ _ are
_ _ im   _ _ im | _ _ ink   _ _ ink | _ _ are   _ _ are
_ _ im | _ _ ink | _ _ are

Spring Training

Read the poem. Circle consonant blends like *str* and consonant trigraphs like *thr* at the beginning of words.

A trigraph is when 3 consonants make a new sound together, like *thr* in *throw*.

Squirt stretches on the mound,

    but Scrappy Sammy's up at bat.

Squirt has thrown straight strikes all day,

a splendid feat at that.

Two strikes whiz by.

Three balls low and away.

As Squirt winds up for the final pitch,

    a strange quiet falls over the play.

The screwball flies toward home.

The bat strikes with a loud, strong *thwack*!

Sammy sprints around the bases,

    and the team goes wild for

Sammy's comeback!

Find and circle **9** objects in this Hidden Pictures® puzzle. Which objects start with a blend?

flute   button   toothbrush   watch   crayon   ruler   mitten

spoon   lollipop

Camp SiGHt Fright

Find and circle at least **20** words with a *gh* combination in this silly story. Say each word as you circle it.

The letters *gh* after vowels change the sounds of the vowels in different ways.

Last night, my neighbor Hugh and I went camping. We set out through the forest. We counted eight different kinds of trees along the rough path. When I thought I could not walk any more, Hugh said he had enough, too. We brought a new tent, but when we started to set it up, the fabric got caught in the zipper. We carefully pulled the fabric out and zipped the tent up to its full height. It was nice and roomy.

In the tent, we each had a yummy doughnut, and I taught Hugh a new card game. All of a sudden, we heard a coughing sound and saw streaks of light. I shook with fright. "We ought to look outside," I told Hugh. We peeked through the flap of the tent, and we had to laugh. A naughty owl stole our flashlight!

Phonics and Spelling: Sounds for Vowels with *GH*

Find and circle **5** objects in this Hidden Pictures® puzzle. What do they all have in common?

| pineapple | banana | lime | pear | apple |

Shhhhhh!

A silent letter isn't spoken when you say the word.

Pssst! There are **21** words with silent letters hidden in this grid. Look for them up, down, across, and diagonally. After you've circled them all, write the leftover letters in order from left to right and top to bottom. They will spell out the answer to the riddle. We've circled the first word to get you started.

BALLET
CLIMB
COMB
DEPOT
GHOST
GNAW
HONEST
HOUR
KNEE
KNIGHT
KNOB

KNOCK
KNOT
LAMB
SWORD
THUMB
TWO
WHALE
WRIST
WRITE
WRONG

C	O	M	B	G	A	P	T	E	H
L	G	N	A	W	N	E	R	L	O
I	O	L	L	R	D	O	A	A	N
M	C	A	L	I	T	Y	R	H	E
B	L	M	E	S	B	E	C	W	S
A	U	B	T	T	S	E	R	T	T
H	K	N	O	C	K	I	E	P	I
T	H	U	M	B	T	W	O	E	S
S	S	A	L	E	O	O	E	W	W
O	A	Y	S	S	N	N	P	I	O
H	O	U	R	L	K	E	K	E	R
G	K	N	I	G	H	T	N	T	D

What is a librarian's favorite prehistoric creature?

_ _ _ _ _ _ _ _ _ _ _ _ _ ,

_ _ _ _ _ _ _ _ _ _ _ _

_ _ _ _ _ _ _ _

_ _ _ _ _ _ _

Words from Words

The letters in **BASKETBALL** can be used to make many other words. Use the clues to fill in the blanks. We filled in the first one to get you started.

BASKETBALL

1. A nighttime creature   <u>B</u> <u>A</u> <u>T</u>
2. Drink it iced or hot.   __ __ __
3. Pose a question.   __ __ __
4. Makes a ringing sound   __ __ __ __
5. Opposite of short   __ __ __ __
6. Pepper's partner   __ __ __ __
7. To put cookies in the oven   __ __ __ __
8. Not early   __ __ __ __
9. The B in BFF   __ __ __ __
10. Huron or Erie   __ __ __ __
11. Direction of a sunrise   __ __ __ __
12. To rollerblade   __ __ __ __ __
13. Opposite of *most*   __ __ __ __ __
14. A horse's home   __ __ __ __ __
15. *The Nutcracker* is one.   __ __ __ __ __ __

Word Ladder

Help the early bird get to the worm! Use the clues to fill in the blanks. Each word is only one letter different from the word above it. We filled in the first one to get you started.

B I R D

1. To tie up — (B) (I) (N) (D)
2. A musical group
3. A magician's stick
4. To wish for something
5. A small, hard lump on the skin
6. Not hot, but not cold

W O R M

All Talk

There are **20** synonyms for *talk* hidden up, down, across, backward, and diagonally in this word search. How many can you find? We circled the first one to get you started.

BABBLE
BELLOW
BLATHER
CRY
EXCLAIM
HISS
HOLLER
JABBER
MUMBLE
MURMUR
PRATTLE
PROCLAIM
RAMBLE
SCREAM
SCREECH
SHRIEK
SPEAK
WHISPER
WHOOP
YELL

```
S P E A K E T R E E I C
Z M U M B L E L L Y W S
S H H E D T X B B E O H
G Y H X W T B V M L L H
P R O C L A I M A L L H
H S L L B R S H R I E K
C C L A A P R M W W B B
E R E I B L A T H E R M
E E R M S H H O I C N C
R A M Q H Z O F S O R D
C M W I Q P V O P I S Y
S E S M J A B B E R H G
M S R U M R U M R E H D
```

Opposite Words

Write the antonym on the blank space beside each word. Once you have them all, read down the column of boxes to find out the answer to the riddle.

WET   __ __ __ __

FAST   __ __ __ __

NOISY   __ __ __ __ __

SOFT   __ __ __ __

ASLEEP   __ __ __ __

WRONG __ __ __ __ __

DIRTY   __ __ __ __ __

What goes up but never comes down?

▢▢▢▢ ▢▢▢

__ __ __ __ __ __ __

Extraordinary

For each word in **bold**, circle the prefix. Underline the original base word. Think about how the prefix changed the meaning of the base word. We did the first one to get you started.

I am so excited to go horseback riding today! Getting on the horse looks **impossible**. What if I am **unable** to climb on? Oh, good, there are stairs to help. We trot in a **semicircle** around the ring. This is **extraordinary**! I feel like a **superstar**. It is time to **return** already. Now how will I **dismount**?

For each word in **bold**, circle the suffix. Underline the original base word. Think about how the suffix changed the meaning of the base word. We did the first one to get you started.

My sister Adva wants to give the horse an apple. The **trainer** says that is okay. Adva has always been **adventurous**. Today she is **fearless**! She holds up the apple and is **careful** to keep her fingers away. The **lovable** horse chomps it up. He enjoys their **friendship**. And she is beaming with **happiness**.

Find and circle **8** objects in this Hidden Pictures® puzzle. What do they all have in common?

rowboat

ruler

radish

rose

racket

raindrop

rocket ship

ring

Time to Rhyme

Rhyming words have the same ending sound.

Across

1. Baseball stick; rhymes with **cat**
3. Banana or apple; rhymes with **toot**
6. Opposite of *yes*; rhymes with **row**
7. A pronoun for a thing; rhymes with **pit**
9. A brief sleep; rhymes with **map**
12. Small child; rhymes with **lot**
14. Unit of weight; rhymes with **jam**
16. To cry hard; rhymes with **cob**
18. Worn around the neck; rhymes with **fly**
19. Icy flakes; rhymes with **grow**
21. Steal; rhymes with **job**
24. A part of the body; rhymes with **hear**
25. A pronoun like *us*; rhymes with **flea**
26. Opposite of *stop*; rhymes with **low**
29. A color name; rhymes with **queen**
30. A female chicken; rhymes with **ten**

Down

1. Use this to catch fish; rhymes with **skate**
2. Opposite of *from*; rhymes with **zoo**
3. A snake's tooth; rhymes with **bang**
4. Opposite of *out*; rhymes with **win**
5. A part of your foot; rhymes with **doe**
8. Throw a ball; rhymes with **gloss**
10. A type of museum; rhymes with **dart**
11. Two of a kind; rhymes with **hair**
13. A musical pitch; rhymes with **cone**
15. A cat sound; rhymes with **sea cow**
17. A type of snake; rhymes with **Noah**
20. A small bird; rhymes with **ten**
22. A vegetable; rhymes with **mean**
23. A breakfast food; rhymes with **leg**
27. Either ___; rhymes with **score**
28. An exclamation; rhymes with **no**

Every clue has a rhyming hint about the word you need to print.
To start things off, we filled in one. Now try the rest and have some fun!

People, Places, Things

Circle the nouns in these sentences. We did the first one to get you started.

The (party) is at my house.

My friends play games.

A clown blows up balloons.

My grandma has a present.

Snacks are on the table.

The cake looks delicious!

Nouns name people, places, and things.

Circle the proper nouns in these sentences. We did the first one to get you started.

(Sally) flies a kite.

Mrs. Johnson reads a book.

Salt City Beach is a busy place!

Maggie points to Ellis Lighthouse.

Jenny and Tom build a sandcastle.

The Snack Shack serves yummy food.

Proper nouns—names of specific people, places, and things—start with uppercase letters.

Can you find **14** shapes or items that appear in both scenes? What people, places, and things (nouns) do you see in each scene?

More Than One

Add **s** to most nouns to make them plural. Add **es** to nouns that end with **s, ch, sh,** or **x.** Read each noun. Make each one plural by adding **s** or **es.** Write the new plural noun.

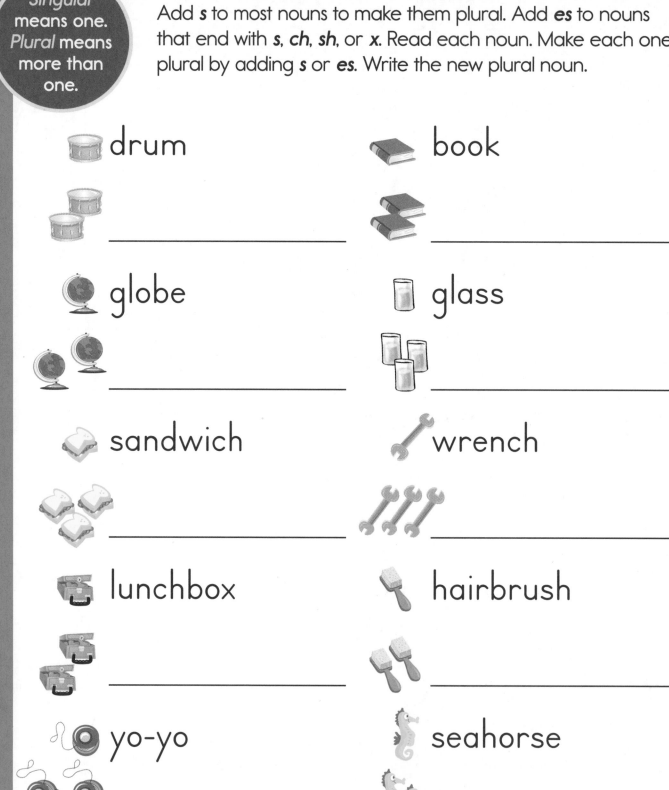

drum

_____

book

_____

globe

_____

glass

_____

sandwich

_____

wrench

_____

lunchbox

_____

hairbrush

_____

yo-yo

_____

seahorse

_____

If a noun ends with a vowel followed by the letter **y**, add **s**. If a noun ends with a consonant followed by the letter **y**, delete the **y** and add **ies**. Read each noun. Decide if you need to add **s** or delete the **y** and add **ies**. Write the plural noun.

key _____

turkey _____

strawberry _____

donkey _____

daisy _____

butterfly _____

Not all nouns follow these rules. Use a dictionary to look up these nouns. Write the plural noun.

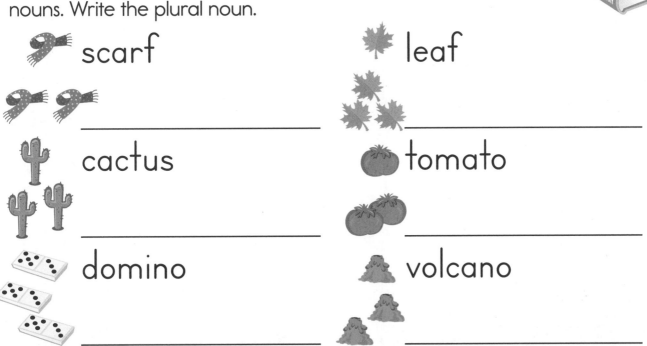

scarf _____

leaf _____

cactus _____

tomato _____

domino _____

volcano _____

Where's My Sheep?

Some nouns that use the same word for singular and plural are *moose*, *fish*, *deer*, and *sheep*.

All the shepherds thought it would be fun to take their sheep to market on the same day, but the leashes got tangled! Follow the lines to see who each sheep belongs to.

Draw a line from the singular to the plural of each noun.

man ○   ○ women

child ○   ○ feet

goose ○   ○ children

mouse ○   ○ oxen

tooth ○   ○ men

woman ○   ○ geese

foot ○   ○ mice

ox ○   ○ teeth

Did You Know?

A group of geese on the ground is called a *gaggle*.

You and Me

Write the pronouns from the word bank to complete the sentences. We filled in the first one to get you started.

He	her	him	I	It	me
~~She~~	them	They	us	We	you

This is Izzy. __She__ has a purple bow.

Can you help _____ solve a math problem?

This is Justin. _____ has a pencil.

Can you help _____ with an art project?

Meet Carly and Ian. _____ both wear

glasses. Can you help _____ answer

a history question?

Tanya is wearing a hat. _____ is red.

What color are _____ wearing?

"I'm Louis. _____ also have a hat.

Can you help _____ read a story?"

"We're Mia and Emily. _____ have

braces. Can you help _____ do a

science experiment?"

Reflections

Write a reflexive pronoun from the word bank to complete the story.

A reflexive pronoun **refers back to the subject of the sentence.**

> herself   himself   itself   myself
> ourselves   themselves   yourself

Yesterday when my family went fishing, we had the dock to _____. Mom bought _____ a new bag to carry all of our gear.

First, Caleb caught a fish all by _____ But when he got too close to the water, Mom had to yell, "Watch _____!"

We saw some ducks sunning _____ on the other side of the pond. One duckling was splashing around, getting _____ wet.

"What a fun day," I thought to _____

as we headed home.

This pond is so still that its surface looks like a mirror. But **8** objects are missing from the reflection. Can you find them?

Grammar: Reflexive Pronouns   59

Whose Smoothie?

A possessive noun **shows** ownership. Make most nouns possessive with **'s.**

Who is drinking each smoothie? Solve the maze, then write the possessive noun to complete each sentence.

Carl   Harper   Jack   Abigail

_____ strawberry smoothie is tasty.

_____ blueberry smoothie is yummy.

_____ orange smoothie is delicious.

_____ banana smoothie is flavorful.

Carl   Harper   Jack   Abigail

My Family

Write the possessive prounouns from the word bank to complete the story.

her His its mine my our Their your

Hi! My name is Mark. This is _____ family. We are making pizza. My sister Olivia is excited. Pizza is _____ favorite food, but _____ is pasta. My baby brother's name is Teddy. He is sitting in the high chair with the toy on _____ tray. _____ favorite food is ice cream. Do you see my mom and dad? _____ favorite food is pasta. All 5 of us agree that _____ favorite drink is milk. What about you? What is _____ favorite food?

What silly things do you see?

Verb Machine

Read each present-tense verb. Add **ed** to make it past tense. If a verb ends in silent **e**, add **d** to make it past tense. Write the new past-tense verb.

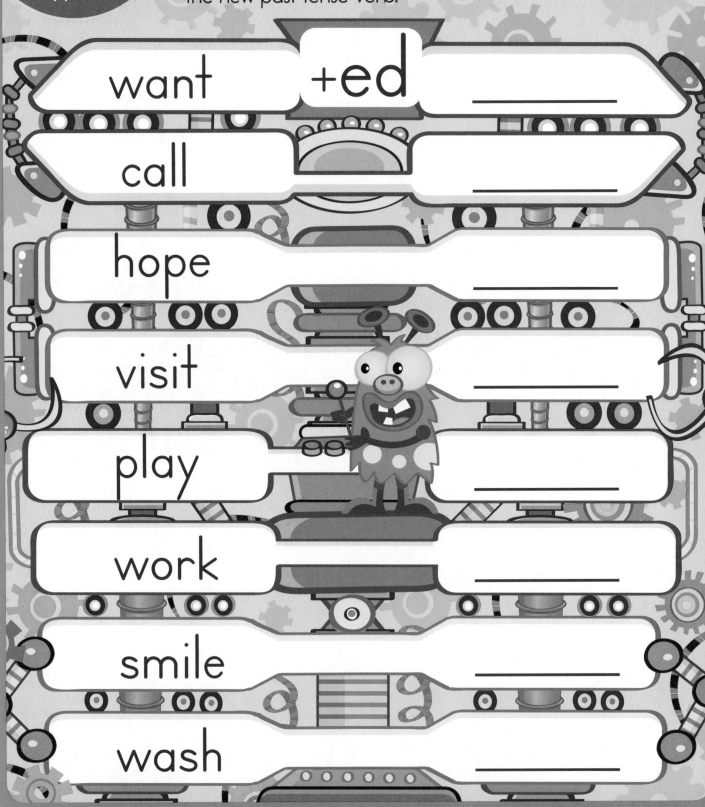

want +ed _____

call _____

hope _____

visit _____

play _____

work _____

smile _____

wash _____

Read each past-tense verb. Delete **ed** or **d**. Write the new present-tense verb.

walked   –ed   _____

cooked   _____

jumped   _____

baked   _____

watched   _____

laughed   _____

arrived   _____

talked   _____

Silly Treehouse

Irregular verbs become different words in the past tense.

Write the past-tense verb from the word bank for each verb shown to complete these sentences about the picture on the next page. We filled in the first one to get you started.

> ate   caught   fell   got   grew   hid
> hung   ran   rose   sat   saw
> slept   stood   swam   told

The boy (eat) _____ ate _____ an ice-cream cone.

One dog (catch) _____ the ball.

Another dog (stand) _____ on the swing.

The shark (swim) _____ in the water.

The squirrel (tell) _____ his friend a story.

A girl (run) _____ by the ladder.

Bushes (grow) _____ in the ground.

The owl (sit) _____ on the boat.

A pail of fruit (hang) _____ from the tree.

A cookie (fall) _____ from the bucket.

An alien (get) _____ lost.

A bee (hide) _____ behind the tree.

The penguin (see) _____ the girl.

A bird (sleep) _____ in his cage.

Smoke (rise) _____ from the chimney.

What silly things do you see? Use the past-tense verb for *throw* to describe what the shark did to the ball. Use the past-tense verb for *sing* to describe what the bird did in his cage.

Try to say this tongue twister five times, fast!

Ron ran past tents in the past tense.

Splashing Around

Write the *ing* verb for each verb shown to complete the story about the picture on the next page. We filled in the first one to get you started.

It's a sunny day at the pig pool. Pigs are (jump) _____jumping_____, (swim) _____, and (play) _____ in the mud. Other pigs are (sit) _____ on towels, (run) _____, and (smile) _____. Can you find the pig that is (read) _____ a book? How many are (eat) _____ ice cream? Can you spot the pig that is (wear) _____ a polka-dotted bathing suit?

Whether they are (splash) _____ in the pool or (relax) _____ by the side, all the pigs are (have) _____ a wonderful time.

baseball bat

flashlight

hockey stick

artist's brush

sailboat

sock

mallet

mitten

ruler

broccoli

purse

ice-cream bar

nail

feather

crescent moon

Find and circle **15** objects in this Hidden Pictures® puzzle. What *ing* verbs can you use to describe how you solved the puzzle?

It's a Maze!

Replace each pair of words shown with a contraction to complete the story.

(I would) _____ like to read a new book today, so (I am) _____ visiting the library. There are lots of books here, and it (is not) _____ hard to find something (you will) _____ really like. First, (I will) _____ check to see if (there is) _____ anything new from my favorite author. (He has) _____ written 3 books that I love. (It is) _____ quiet here so people can read, so I (should not) _____ make too much noise. I pass a man (who is) _____ drinking tea and a woman looking at the shelves. I think (she is) _____ having trouble finding the book she wants. I (can not) _____ decide on one book, so (I have) _____ picked 12 to bring home. (They are) _____ heavy, so my friend offers to help. (We are) _____ going to carry 6 books each to the check-out desk.

Mark has a tall stack of books to check out at the library, but he can't see over his pile. Help him find a way to the check-out desk.

Adjectives are words that describe nouns.

Circle the adjectives in this story. Can you find **19**?

When fall comes, I am a happy kid. The air is cold. The leaves are colorful. And I go on fun trips with my class. Yesterday, we went to an old cider mill, where we learned how to make fresh cider. The workers take crisp, red apples, squeeze out the sweet juice with a special machine, and make tasty cider. The mill also makes warm doughnuts. They are sugary and delicious. Before we left, I picked an orange pumpkin to bring home. My friend wanted a tall pumpkin, but I chose a big, round one. I'll carve a scary face on it for Halloween!

muffin

jar

frog

button

pear

spoon

cane

pencil

horseshoe

ruler

glove

crescent moon

wishbone

sock

slice of pizza

Find and circle **15** objects in this Hidden Pictures® puzzle. What adjective could you use to describe each object?

Comparing Animals

Animals come in all shapes and sizes! Write the comparative and superlative forms of each **bold** adjective to describe the animals on the next page.

Add *er* to make most comparative adjectives, which compare two things. Add *est* to make most superlative adjectives, which compare three or more things.

The mice are **small**. They are _____ than the meerkats. They are the _____ animals.

The giraffe is **tall**. She is _____ than the elephant. She is the _____ animal.

The birds are **bright**. They are _____ than the rhinoceros. They are the _____ animals.

If the adjective ends in *e*, just add *r* or *st*. If the adjective ends in *y*, change the *y* to an *i* before adding *er* or *est*, as in *shiny*, *shinier*, and *shiniest*.

The elephant is **large**. He is _____ than the lions. He is the _____ animal.

The monkey is **silly**. She is _____ than the rhinoceros. She is the _____ animal.

The lion is **hairy**. He is _____ than the warthog. He is the _____ animal.

What animal wears the biggest shoes?

The one with the biggest feet

Find and circle **12** objects in this Hidden Pictures® puzzle.

heart

slice of pie

shoe

fish

comb

mitten

ice-cream cone

sailboat

slice of pizza

bird

bell

fishhook

73

Win or Lose

A conjunction can join words, phrases, and parts of sentences. Some conjunctions can change the meaning of the sentence.

Write a conjunction from the word bank to join the two parts of these sentences.

| and | because | but | so | or |

My friends _____ I are on an ice hockey team. There are 20 kids on the team, _____ only 6 play at a time.

I wear a helmet _____ my head will be safe. We like to play _____ it is fun. We have fun if we win _____ if we lose.

How many hockey sticks can you find in this picture?

74   Grammar: Conjunctions

A, An, and The

The 3 articles are *a*, *an*, and *the*.

A and *an* are **indefinite articles**. They are used to refer to 1 of something. Use *a* before a singular noun that begins with a consonant sound. Use *an* before a singular noun that begins with a vowel sound.

The is a **definite article**. Use *the* before plural nouns and nouns that refer to something specific.

Circle the article before each noun to complete the story.

Today my family went to (an/the) zoo. I wanted to see (a/an) elephant, and my sister wanted to see (a/an) lion. Our favorite animals were (a/the) penguins. We took (a/an) picture with (an/the) camera. Then I ate (a/an) ice-cream cone. It was (a/an/the) best day ever!

What is your favorite zoo animal? Draw a picture of it here.

At Silly Park

Some prepositions show position.

Write the prepositions from the word bank to complete the story about the picture on the next page.

| across | at | behind | between |
| in front of | | next to | on under |

I saw the strangest things _____ the park today! A gorilla was sitting _____ the bench reading a book. My friend Jasper was sitting _____ him. Just then, a penguin jumped _____ two girls playing catch. I couldn't believe my eyes when I spotted a lizard on a leash with a dog _____ it. They were walking _____ the jungle gym. As I walked _____ the river to head home, a dragon swam _____ the bridge. What a silly day!

What silly things do you see? What preposition can you use to describe the position of the cat? What preposition can you use to describe the position of the doughnuts?

How? When? Where?

Adverbs can answer questions about how an action was done. Write the adverbs from the word bank under the questions they answer. We filled in the first one to get you started.

~~always~~   here   inside   never   now   outside
quickly   quietly   slowly   soon   today   twice

How?

_____

_____

How Often?

always

_____

_____

When?

_____

_____

Where?

_____

_____

Many adjectives can be changed to adverbs by adding *ly*. If the adjective ends in *y*, delete the *y* and add *ily*. If the adjective ends in *le*, replace the *e* with *y*. Turn the adjectives shown here into adverbs to complete the story.

My grandpa took me and my cousins fishing. The sun was shining (warm) _____ in the sky. Ducks drifted (gentle) _____ by us. And we sat (quiet) _____ with our rods. Well, not all of us. My cousin Kaycee (noisy) _____ munched on a sandwich. But that didn't scare off the fish. One was on Grandpa's line! My brother (quick) _____ caught it in the net. I had something on my line, too. I (slow) _____ reeled it in, but guess what was on the hook? An old boot. I would (happy) _____ eat fish for dinner, but not soggy shoes!

Find the words (not pictures) BAIT, CANOE, MOUNTAIN, NET, and PINE hidden in the scene.

Trace and write the cursive A's.

𝒜 𝒶 𝒜 𝒶

Trace the sentence.

Anna is an amazing artist.

The names of **17** kinds of apples are hidden up, down, across, backward, and diagonally in this word search. We found BALDWIN. Can you find the rest? When you've found them all, look for **4** wiggling WORMs hiding in the apple.

WORD LIST

~~BALDWIN~~
BRAEBURN
CORTLAND
CRISPIN
DELICIOUS
EMPIRE
FUJI
GALA
GRANNY SMITH
IDARED
JONATHAN
MCINTOSH
MUTSU
PAULA RED
PIPPIN
ROME
WINESAP

Handwriting: Cursive A *a*

Trace and write the cursive B's.

Trace the sentence.

Help Bradley Beetle find his friends in the middle of the maze.

Cc

Trace and write the cursive C's.

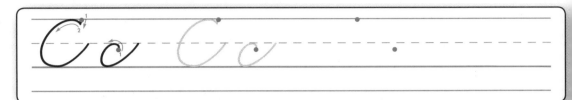

Trace the sentence.

Casey wears a cap and cape.

Find the matching pairs of cats.

Trace and write the cursive D's.

Trace the sentence.

Dave pounds the drum.

How many dinosaurs can you find in this room?

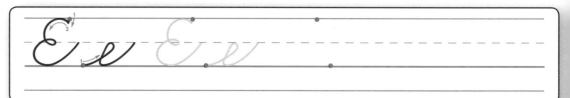

Trace and write the cursive E's.

Trace the sentence.

Emily gets eggs every day.

The elephant hears with very big ears. Draw a picture of what he's listening to here.

Handwriting: Cursive *E e*

Trace and write the cursive F's.

Trace the sentence.

Use the frog code to fill in the letters and finish the jokes.

| A | C | D | E | H | I | K |

| L | N | O | P | R | S | Y |

What did the bus driver say to the frog?

"_____ _____ _____ _____ _____!"

Where do frogs take notes?

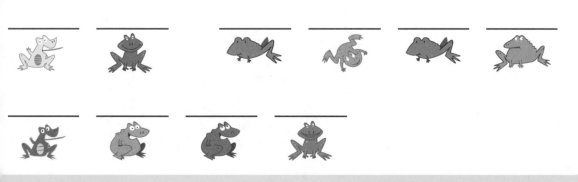

$\mathscr{G}g$

Trace and write the cursive G's.

Trace the sentence.

Gigi makes a goofy ghost.

Draw a path to get the golf ball into the lion's mouth.

Handwriting: Cursive G g

Trace and write the cursive H's.

 $\mathcal{H}$ h $\mathcal{H}$ h

Trace the sentence.

Harry holds
a huge horn.

Follow the steps to draw a horse, or draw one from your imagination.

1.
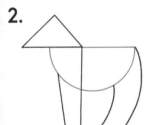

2.

3.

4.

Trace and write the cursive *I*'s.

Trace the sentence.

Iris glides on ice skates.

The names of **16** insects are hidden down and across in this word search. We found ANT. Can you find the rest?

WORD LIST
- ~~ANT~~
- APHID
- BEETLE
- BUTTERFLY
- CRICKET
- DRAGONFLY
- FIREFLY
- FLEA
- GNAT
- HONEYBEE
- HOUSEFLY
- LADYBUG
- LOUSE
- MOTH
- TERMITE
- WASP

```
D R A G O N F L Y X
C M O T H B I Z Q J
R B U T T E R F L Y
I X V Z W E E J T L
C Q G N A T F L E A
K A N T S L L O R D
E V Z J P E Y U M Y
T Z A P H I D S I B
H O N E Y B E E T U
H O U S E F L Y E G
```

Trace and write the cursive J's.

Trace the sentence.

Jeff wears a

jazzy jacket.

· ·

These two juggling scenes are exactly alike except for one difference. Can you find it?

K k

Trace and write the cursive K's.

Trace the sentence.

Keiko likes the kitten.

Find and circle the two kites that are the same.

Trace and write the cursive L's.

Trace the sentence.

Lila and Leo are ready for lunch. Draw a clear path through the leaves to their home.

M m

Trace and write the cursive M's.

Trace the sentence.

Mimi marches to music.

Maya, Marco, and Mom are making muffins. Can you find **11 M**'s hidden in this scene?

Two muffins are sitting in an oven.

MUFFIN 1: *Does it feel warm in here to you?*

MUFFIN 2: *AAH! A talking muffin!*

Trace and write the cursive N's.

Trace the sentence.

Nina notices a note.

· ·

Follow these steps to make a newspaper hat.

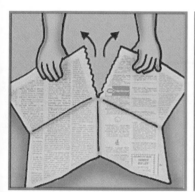

1. Tear a page of newspaper in half.

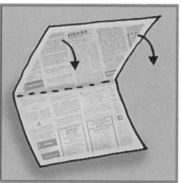

2. Fold one of the pieces in half.

3. Fold the top corners down.

4. Fold the bottom bands up.

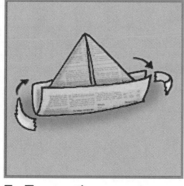

5. Tape the corners of the band.

6. Decorate your hat.

O o

Trace and write the cursive O's.

Trace the sentence.

Owen looks at the owl.

Fill in this grid with the O words listed below. Use the number of letters in each word as a clue to where it might fit. We did one to get you started.

O
A
R

WORD LIST

OAR
ONE
OWL
OBOE
OVAL
OVEN
OCEAN
OLIVE
ONION
ORANGE
OCTAGON
OCTOPUS
OVERALLS

Trace and write the cursive P's.

Trace the sentence.

Connect the dots from 1 to 25 to find a popular treat that starts with p.

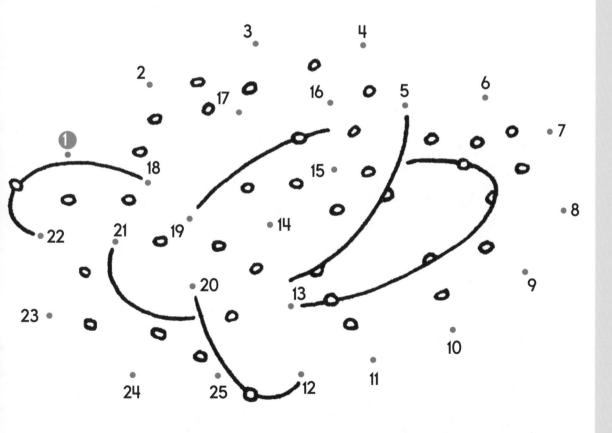

Qq

Trace and write the cursive Q's.

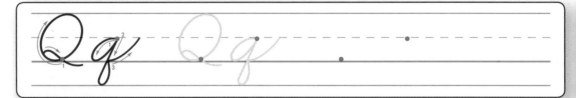

Trace the sentence.

Quincy wants quiet quickly!

Find your way through the quilt on the white path from START to FINISH.

START

FINISH

Trace and write the cursive **R**'s.

Trace the sentence.

Ryan and Roy
ride bikes.

Each of these robots has something in common with the other 2 robots in the same row. For example, in the first row across, all 3 robots are on wheels. Look at the other rows across, down, and diagonally. Can you tell what is alike in each row?

Trace and write the cursive S's.

Trace the sentence.

Sam slurps a snow cone.

There are stars all over at Sasha's skateboarding party.
Can you find all 15?

What's the hardest part about learning to skateboard?

The pavement

Trace and write the cursive T's.

Trace the sentence.

Help Trent find the trowel he lost while planting tulips.

What flowers grow between your nose and chin?

Tulips (two lips)

START

FINISH

U u

Trace and write the cursive U's.

U u U u

Trace the sentence.

Una is under the umbrella.

Each row and column has **2** extra utensils. Cross out the extras so that every row and column contains just **1** fork, **1** spoon, and **1** knife.

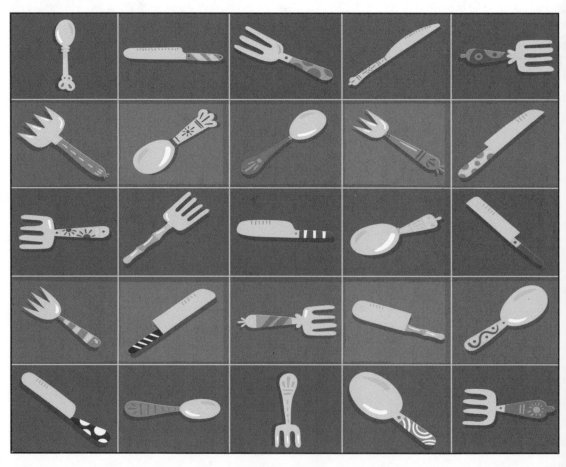

Trace and write the cursive V's.

Trace the sentence.

The names of **18** vegetables are hidden down and across in this word search. We found BEANS to get you started. Can you find the rest?

```
C A B B A G E Z W B
E G G P L A N T C E
L V P O T A T O U A
E K O N I O N B C N
R A D I S H F E U S
Y L E T T U C E M Q
P E P P E R C T B U
M U S H R O O M E A
C A R R O T R X R S
P E A S P I N A C H
```

WORD LIST

~~BEANS~~
BEET
CABBAGE
CARROT
CELERY
CORN
CUCUMBER
EGGPLANT
KALE
LETTUCE
MUSHROOM
ONION
PEAS
PEPPER
POTATO
RADISH
SPINACH
SQUASH

Handwriting: Cursive V v

Ww

Trace and write the cursive W's.

Trace the sentence.

Wesley wants to write.

Write the winter word that starts with "snow" in each of these word combos.

Handwriting: Cursive W w

Trace and write the cursive **X**'s.

$\mathcal{X}x$

Trace the sentence.

Xandi plays the xylophone

Fill in this grid with the **21** words listed below. Use the number of letters in each word as a clue to where it might fit. We did the first one to get you started.

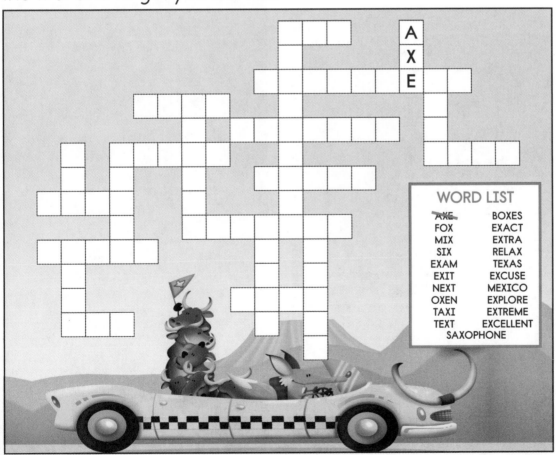

WORD LIST

AXE	BOXES
FOX	EXACT
MIX	EXTRA
SIX	RELAX
EXAM	TEXAS
EXIT	EXCUSE
NEXT	MEXICO
OXEN	EXPLORE
TAXI	EXTREME
TEXT	EXCELLENT
SAXOPHONE	

Y y

Trace and write the cursive Y's.

Trace the sentence.

Yuri makes yummy pops.

Danny and Manny are yo-yo experts. Find and circle 10 differences between these pictures.

Trace and write the cursive Z's.

Trace the sentence.

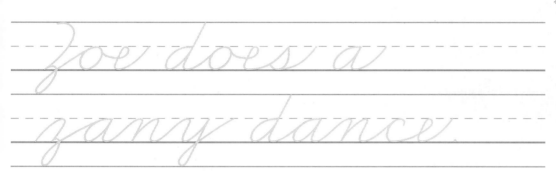

Zoe does a zany dance.

Follow each path to see where each group is going at the zoo.

Storm Magic

Annie looked at the rain outside.
"I wish we could play on the swings."

"Not until the rain stops," Grandma said.

"Let's practice magic tricks," said Katy.

They found a pencil, a bead, a cup, and a scarf. Annie made the pencil stick to her hand. Katy dropped the bead into the cup, and the bead disappeared. But the girls got tangled in the scarf.

Grandma clapped. "Good show!"

"Look!" Katy said. She pointed out the window.

"The storm made magic, too!" said Annie. "First the sun disappeared. Now the sun is back. And it brought a rainbow!"

1. At the beginning of the story, it is

   ○ raining.   ○ snowing.   ○ sunny.

2. How do the girls feel about the weather?

   ○ excited   ○ disappointed   ○ angry

3. Who suggests practicing tricks?

   ○ Katy   ○ Annie   ○ Grandma

4. Which thing did the girls not use for their magic tricks?

   ○ pencil   ○ scarf   ○ straw

5. Where did the girls see the sun?

   ○ out the door   ○ out the window   ○ on TV

6. What do you think happens next?

   ○ The girls play on the swings.

   ○ The girls watch TV.   ○ The girls have dinner.

Sun and Wind

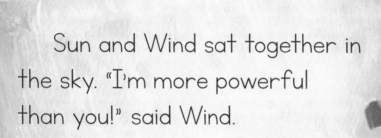

Sun and Wind sat together in the sky. "I'm more powerful than you!" said Wind.

"I don't think so," said Sun.

"See that boy in the hat?" said Wind. "Let's see who can get his hat to come off." Wind blew and blew. The boy shivered and held on to his hat.

Sun said, "I'll try." Sun simply smiled down on the boy. Soon the boy was so warm that he took his hat off.

"A warm smile is often more powerful than a blast of wind," said Sun.

1. Who is arguing?

_____

2. What does the boy do when Wind blows?

_____

3. When does the boy finally take off his hat?

_____

4. Where are Sun and Wind?

_____

5. Why does the boy finally take off his hat?

_____

6. How does Sun make the boy warm?

_____

Impossible to Train

"Is your pet hard to train?" asked Jesse.

Sammy sighed. "He's hopeless. He can't learn anything properly."

"You should see my pet when we go for walks," said Bea. "Always pulling on the leash. He's seriously strange."

"You should see mine when we play a stick-throwing game," said Sammy. "We have this big tug-of-war with the stick. He's seriously silly!"

"You should see mine when we go swimming," Jesse said. "She goes splashing around in big circles. She's seriously embarrassing!"

"I wonder if anyone has a pet as silly as mine," said Sammy.

"I wonder if anyone has a pet as strange as mine," said Bea.

"I wonder if anyone has a pet as embarrassing as mine," said Jesse.

"Mine does try hard," Sammy said after a moment. "He's good about eating. He doesn't leave bits of food on the floor for me to clean up."

Jesse nodded. "Mine is friendly. She likes to play, and she never sulks. But she's so hard to train!" Jesse said.

Bea sighed, "Our pets will never learn."

Jesse woofed in agreement. Sammy thumped his tail.

"Humans!" said Jesse. "Impossible to train, but we love them anyway."

1. Who is talking in this story?

   ○ kids   ○ dogs   ○ trees

2. How do the speakers in this story feel about their pets?

   _____

3. Who says "He can't learn anything properly"?

   _____

4. Who says "I wonder if anyone has a pet as silly as mine"?

   _____

5. Why is this story funny?

   _____

   _____

6. What do you imagine your pet thinks about you?

   _____

   _____

Too Many Bags!

Rabbit had too many plastic shopping bags. They tumbled out of his cabinet. "I have to clean this mess," Rabbit said.

"I can help you," said Raccoon. "But I need some scissors and tape."

Rabbit gave Raccoon scissors and tape. "Are you going to tape my cabinet doors shut?" Rabbit asked.

Raccoon laughed. "No." She put an armful of bags on the table.

Snip. Snip. Raccoon cut the handles off each bag. *Snip. Snip.* Raccoon cut along the sides of each bag so that the bag formed one big strip.

Rabbit stared at the pile of strips.

"This mess is getting bigger!"

Raccoon smiled. She took three strips and tied their ends into a knot. Then she braided the strips together. At the end of the braid, she taped on new strips. Soon, Raccoon had turned the whole pile of strips into one long rope.

"It's a jump rope!" Rabbit cheered.

Raccoon smiled. "Yes! Now we can go outside and play jump-rope games."

"I'll get my shoes," Rabbit said. He opened his closet door, and a tower of boxes tumbled out. "Can you help me with this problem, too?" he asked Raccoon.

1. Where are Rabbit and Racoon?

_____

2. Which word best describes Rabbit?

    ○ disorganized   ○ neat   ○ funny

3. Which word best describes Raccoon?

    ○ unhelpful   ○ helpful   ○ worried

4. What problem does Rabbit have?

_____

5. How does Raccoon solve that problem?

_____

_____

_____

The Mysterious Manor

"This house always gives me the creeps," said Priyanka as she and Dan passed the blue house on the corner. They walked by it every day on their way to and from school. Nobody had lived there in years.

"My brother says it's not a house at all," said Dan as he ran his fingers along the iron fence that surrounded the yard. "He says it's really a magic portal."

"Do you really think if you walk in the door, you can be transported to another place and time?" asked Priyanka.

Just then, the door on the house burst open and . . .

Read the beginning of the story. Can you imagine what happens next? Write your own ending to the story.

_____

_____

_____

_____

_____

_____

_____

_____

_____

_____

_____

_____

Warm Welcome

Welcome, earthworm in the dirt.
Welcome, inchworm on my shirt.
Welcome, sparrows in the trees.
Welcome, busy bumblebees.
Welcome, itty-bitty fly.
Welcome, bunny hopping by.
Welcome, bullfrog standing guard.
Welcome to my big backyard.

1. Who is talking in the poem?

   o a boy   o a fly   o a frog

2. What word is repeated 8 times in the poem?

   _____

3. Which word in the poem rhymes with
   dirt? _____ With _trees_? _____
   With _fly_? _____
   With _backyard_? _____

4. Find 2 places where words that start with
   _b_ are right next to each other.

   _____

   _____

5. How does the boy feel about nature?

   _____

The King's Challenge

Once, long ago, a wise old king wanted to find a new ruler for his land. Of course, many people thought they should have the crown. They claimed to be the strongest or smartest or richest. The king paid no attention to their boasts. Instead, he announced a challenge. The next ruler would be the one to complete three tasks: catch a thousand fish, train a lion, and find the kingdom's most valuable treasure.

"Impossible," said one man. "Nobody here has a boat that can hold a thousand fish, and a lion can't be trusted."

Another man scowled. "There are no valuable treasures here. When I plow my fields, I find only stones."

A young lady named Jaya didn't complain. She thought about the king's tasks as she walked along the seashore. She stepped over tangles of seaweed and bits of driftwood. She watched fish dart through the water like arrows.

Then she saw something that made her heart leap. She filled a pail and hurried off to the king.

"What have we here?" the king asked.

"They're eggs," Jaya explained. "Each one will become a fish. My bucket holds thousands of them."

The king nodded. "You found a way to catch a thousand fish without a boat. You will need to be very clever to train a lion."

Jaya left the castle and thought about the king's words as she walked along the path near the forest.

A breeze blew, and leaves swirled through the air like butterflies. They whispered a wonderful idea to her.

The next morning, Jaya returned to the castle with a package under her arm.

"Is a lion hidden in that paper?" asked the king as Jaya bowed before him.

"Yes," she said. "But I must free it outside."

In the courtyard, Jaya opened the package and unwrapped a large kite. She sprinted across the ground. A glorious lion kite soared into the sky. Jaya pulled the strings, and it twirled and danced and dipped through the clouds.

"I've trained my lion to dance for you," said Jaya.

"You are very clever," said the king. "But you will need eyes that see everything to find the most valuable treasure in the kingdom."

Walking home along cobbled streets, Jaya thought about the king's words. She stared into shop windows. When the baker gave her a muffin, Jaya had a delicious idea.

The next morning, Jaya stood at the castle door. This time, she brought a crowd with her.

"I don't see glimmering gold or sparkling rubies," said the king.

"That's because the *people* are the kingdom's most valuable treasure," Jaya replied. "They share their talents and make everyone happy. We have the potter's vases, the musicians' songs, the tailor's slippers, and the baker's muffins."

The king smiled. "Your answer shows me you will be a wise queen. You are patient and clever. But most important, you know that the people around you are the true riches of the kingdom. I'm sure you'll take good care of them." Then he stepped forward and handed Jaya the crown.

These are some parts of the plot of "The King's Challenge." Fill in the circle by "beginning," "middle," or "end" to tell when each event happened in the story. Select the answer to the last question.

1. Jaya flies a lion kite in the sky and makes it "dance" for the king.

   ○ Beginning   ○ Middle   ○ End

2. Jaya brings many people to the king since they are "the kingdom's most valuable treasure."

   ○ Beginning   ○ Middle   ○ End

3. The king announces he must find a new ruler and asks people to perform three tasks.

   ○ Beginning   ○ Middle   ○ End

4. Jaya collects fish eggs as a way to "catch a thousand fish."

   ○ Beginning   ○ Middle   ○ End

5. The king tells Jaya that she will be a wise queen and gives her a crown.

   ○ Beginning   ○ Middle   ○ End

6. Which theme best describes the lesson of "The King's Challenge"?

   ○ Help other people   ○ Overcome challenges
   ○ Share with others

The Perfect Job for Odo

Odo was the fastest kite maker at the Kwiggley Kite Factory.

One day, Odo stopped.

While Odo ate his lunch in the park, he read job ads.

Read this graphic story. A graphic story includes illustrations that follow the sequence of events.. When you are finished, answer the questions on page 125.

He rushed over to Megastar Studios.
The waiting room was crowded.

Finally, his turn came.

*I'll find a new job tomorrow,
Odo thought.*

The next morning,
Odo stopped at the diner.

Odo tried to keep up, but the orders came too fast.

Isn't there any job that's right for me?

Then he heard a small cry. And more cries.

Odo dashed inside.

Odo rocked all the babies to sleep.

1. In "The Perfect Job for Odo," the narration of the story appears

   ○ in speech bubbles.   ○ under each scene.
   ○ nowhere because there is no narration.

2. The main character in the story is

   ○ Nurse Robin.   ○ Odo.   ○ Mr. Kwiggley.

3. What problem does Odo have at the beginning of the story?

   _____

4. How does Odo try to solve his problem in the middle of the story?

   _____

5. How does Odo finally solve his problem at the end of the story?

   _____

6. How did the illustrations help you better understand "The Perfect Job for Odo"?

   _____

Butterflies in Disguise

The picture below shows the Question Mark butterfly with its wings open.

When the insect flashes these bright colors, it lets other butterflies know where it is.

The picture at right shows the same butterfly resting with its wings up.

Now the butterfly looks like a leaf or a rock or a piece of tree bark. A hungry bird may not even see the butterfly!

This dull coloring, which helps the butterfly blend in with its surroundings, is called *camouflage*. Many other butterflies also have camouflage on the bottom of their wings.

Read the essay about butterflies. Then answer the questions.

1. A butterfly is
   ○ a mammal.   ○ a reptile.   ○ an insect.

2. The Question Mark butterfly shows its colors to signal to
   ○ predators.   ○ people.   ○ other butterflies.

3. The side of its wings with the dull colors helps the butterfly
   ○ fly faster.   ○ catch bugs.   ○ hide from predators.

4. What does the word "camouflage" mean?
   ○ the ability to blend into the surrounding area
   ○ a hood that camels need to wear
   ○ a flag that you wave at parades

Can you match each camouflaged butterfly to its brightly colored self?
Look at the shape of each butterfly's wing if you need a hint.

A ○   ○ 1

B ○   ○ 2

C ○   ○ 3

Bubble Bonanza

Make a BIG-BUBBLE WAND

1. Cut a length of yarn or cotton string so it's six times as long as a plastic drinking straw.

2. Thread the string through two plastic straws.

3. Tie the ends of the string together. Slide the knot inside one of the straws.

Using the straw pieces as handles, dunk the wand into the bubble solution to coat the straws and string. (Wet your hands, too.) Hold the straws together as you lift them out. Pull them apart slowly to make a sheet of bubble film. Pull the wand through the air. Bring the straws together to close the bubble.

Stir Up a Super Bubble Solution

1. Put 3 cups of "**soft**" or **distilled water** in a clean bucket.

2. Add 6 tablespoons of **dish detergent** (Dawn works well) and 3 tablespoons of **glycerin** or **corn syrup**. Corn syrup and glycerin make the soap film stronger.

3. Gently stir the ingredients. Try not to create suds.

4. Let the mixture sit for a few hours or overnight before using it. This lets the ingredients combine well and gives any bits of dirt a chance to settle out of the solution.

1. What are the ingredients for bubble solution?

    _____

2. To make bubble solution, what do you do first?

    _____

    _____

3. What is the last step to making bubble solution?

    _____

    _____

4. How many steps will it take to make a big-bubble wand?

    _____

5. How many straws do you need to make a big-bubble wand?

    _____

6. How long should the yarn or cotton string be for the wand?

    _____

129

Rubeosaurus/Tyrannotitan

Tyrannotitan
tie-RAN-oh-TIE-ten
"giant tyrant"

Tyrannotitan is the earliest-known big meat eater, and lived south of the equator, in Argentina. Growing to 40 feet in length, this giant of the Cretaceous period hunted alone, using its long claws and saw-edged teeth to prey on other dinosaurs. Like all dinosaurs, *Tyrannotitan* hatched from eggs.

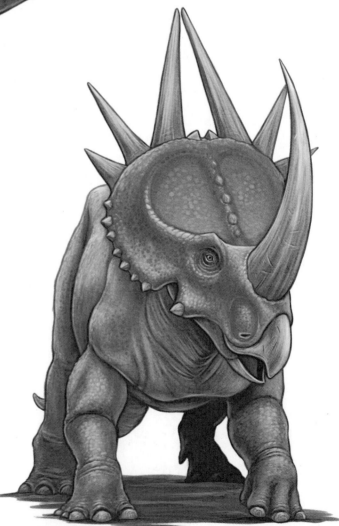

Rubeosaurus
roo-BAY-oh-SAWR-us
"thornbush lizard"

Rubeosaurus was a dinosaur that roamed the state of Montana during the Cretaceous period. Herds of *Rubeosaurus* traveled together, eating leaves and young plants. Individuals could grow to 12 feet in length, and used their spiky horns to defend against predators.

Read the descriptions and look at the drawings of *Rubeosaurus* and *Tyrannotitan*. Draw a line from each fact below to the correct box to see what is the same and what is different about the two dinosaurs.

Meat-eater

Plant-eater

40 feet long

12 feet long

Bones found in the United States

Bones found in South America

Horned

No horns

Babies hatch from eggs

Lived in herds

Lived alone

Lived in the Cretaceous period

Thick, strong back legs

Tyrannotitan

Both

Rubeosaurus

Chasing Chickens

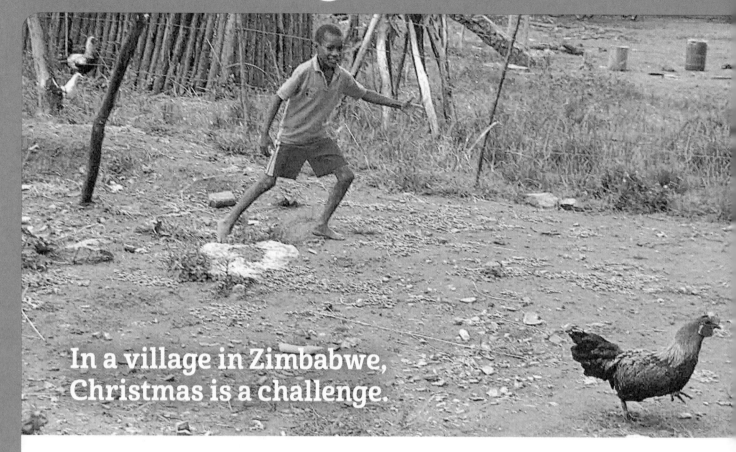

In a village in Zimbabwe, Christmas is a challenge.

When I arrive in the village of Cheziya early on December 25, there is nothing to remind me that it is Christmas. I do not see any trees or lights. Not a single child I see has a present.

This is not really surprising to me. Cheziya is a village far away from other towns and villages, and there is little money for presents.

But I am about to learn that Christmas is still special in this village. It is the day of the annual Christmas Chicken Chase Challenge.

The Best Chicken Chasers

Chickens are common in Cheziya. Every homestead seems to have some chickens running around, feeding on scraps and grains. But most families eat them only on special occasions. And Christmas is a special occasion. Every family in this village will have a chicken on the table for dinner.

But first, the villagers hold a challenge to see who is the best chicken catcher.

"Not every kid in the village qualifies for the challenge," explains Edward Majoni, the referee of the contest. "We need the kids who have proved to be capable chicken chasers." Eight kids have been chosen this year: three boys and five girls, including Angela, the defending champion from Christmas last year. Six chickens have been selected for today's event.

The rules are simple. The kids chase the selected six chickens. The first to catch one is the winner.

"What is the trophy?" I ask Edward.

"The chicken is the trophy," Edward replies. "The winner gets the whole chicken fried to eat—alone if he or she wishes so."

The Chase Begins

"Now catch your Christmas chicken, boys and girls!" Edward shouts. Then he whistles loudly and the contest begins.

The second Edward whistles, the six chickens take off, mingling with all the other chickens. The kids take off, too, trying to find their targets among all the chickens.

Twelve-year-old Shuvai has a chicken in her sights. One of the hens is standing still in the middle of all the chaos. Shuvai tiptoes silently, hoping to catch the chicken by

chases it into a bush. She emerges a moment later, without a chicken.

Tinaye is tired. He's standing beside a hut when a chicken rushes through the open door. This is his chance. He quickly follows it into the hut. "I got it! I got it!" Tinaye shouts as he walks out of the hut, holding the chicken.

Edward and the other kids congratulate Tinaye. They also want to know if he will eat the chicken alone.

"I am the champion and I have the right to eat as much of it as I can," he says with a broad smile. "Maybe I will share it, since it is Christmas."

surprise. When she is about two feet away, she lunges. But the chicken races away.

Matthew is determined to win the challenge. His strategy is to outrun a chicken. While he is racing after one of the birds, a chicken runs straight at Angela. She stands still and prepares to catch it. Suddenly, the chicken runs in the other direction. Angela

1. **Where** does the chicken challenge take place?

_____

2. **When** in the year does the author visit the village?

_____

3. **How** does the referee signal the start of the challenge?

_____

4. **Who** catches the chicken? How does he do it?

_____

_____

What is the meaning of the underlined word in each sentence from the story?

5. "It is the day of the <u>annual</u> Christmas Chicken Chase Challenge."

     o special   o yearly   o past

6. "But most families eat them only on special <u>occasions</u>."

     o events   o tables   o jobs

7. "His <u>strategy</u> is to outrun a chicken."

     o goal   o plan   o game

Subway Subjects

Look at the pictures on the next page. Write each subject or verb from the word banks to complete each sentence.

| beaver | crocodile | snake | turtle |

The _____ stands.

The _____ holds on.

The _____ hisses.

The _____ smiles.

| swings | sleeps | listens | reads |

The goat _____.

The elephant _____.

The bear _____.

The monkey _____.

Find at least 18 differences between these two pictures.

Carnival Objects

Unscramble these sentences to follow the pattern *subject–verb–object*. Don't forget to capitalize the first word and add a punctuation mark at the end of each sentence.

cotton candy holds Julie

_____

throws balls Tim

_____

Eli ice cream eats

_____

waves a flag he

_____

munch popcorn I

_____

a man balloons holds

_____

tickets sells who

_____

Katie coaster rides the

_____

There are 6 words (not pictures) hidden in this scene. Can you find CANDY, GAMES, PRIZE, RIDE, TICKETS, and WIN? Which of these words can be both a verb and a noun?

Library Statements

Look at the scene on the next page. Write 7 statements to describe something or tell what someone is doing. Remember that each statement starts with an uppercase letter and ends with a period. We did one to get you started.

The librarian reads a story.

Find and circle **9** objects in this Hidden Pictures® puzzle. Then write a statement about the hidden object you found first.

| spoon | glove | baseball bat | crescent moon | carrot | butterfly | bat | fish | ruler |

Bus-Stop Questions

A question ends with a question mark. It is a sentence that asks something.

Look at the maze on the next page. Write 7 questions about it beginning with these question words. Put a question mark at the end of each sentence. We did the first one to get you started.

Who _waits at the bus stop?_

What _____

Where _____

When _____

Why _____

How _____

Which _____

The bus has one more stop before getting to school. Pick up the kids waiting at the bus stop, then find the way to school. How do you get to school?

Scrambled Exclamations

Grammar: Write Exclamations

What a noisy party! But the sounds are all mixed up. Unscramble each sound. Then write a new sentence for each sound. See how many exclamation points you can use. We did the first one to get you started.

ACHOO! That was a loud sneeze!

_____

_____

_____

_____

_____

_____

_____

_____

_____

_____

_____

_____

Make a Pizza

Here's a fun recipe for mini-pizza. Before you start cooking, circle the verb in each of the 6 instructions. Then write your own recipe using commands on a separate sheet of paper.

1. Preheat the oven to 375 degrees Fahrenheit with a parent's help.

2. Toast an **English muffin**.

3. Place the toasted English muffin on a baking sheet, toasted side up.

4. Spread **pizza sauce** over the English muffin.

5. Top the English muffin with **shredded mozzarella cheese** and whatever toppings you want.

6. Bake the pizza in the oven for 10 minutes with a parent's help.

Find and circle **12** objects in this Hidden Pictures® scene. How would you tell someone how to use a toothbrush? How would you tell someone how to use a yo-yo?

sock

canoe

fish

ring

comb

artist's brush

drinking straw

toothbrush

hockey stick

baseball

pennant

yo-yo

Sorting Sentences

There are 4 kinds of sentences: statements, commands, questions, and exclamations.

Read these sentences. Draw a line from each sentence to the box that names the type of sentence.

STATEMENT

I love my cat.

Where does this flower grow?

COMMAND

Feed my cat.

What is my cat doing?

QUESTION

My cat is so beautiful!

The flower is pretty.

EXCLAMATION

Smell the flower.

This flower is gigantic!

Find and circle **9** objects in this Hidden Pictures® puzzle. What type of sentence would you use to tell where you found the scissors? What type of sentence would you use to ask for help finding the ring?

slice of pizza

crown

rocket ship

toothbrush

toast

scissors

envelope

bell

ring

Loose Lizard

Rewrite each sentence. Use an uppercase letter at the beginning and a period, question mark, or exclamation point at the end.

that lizard is loose

_____

the turtle is green

_____

how did the lizard get away

_____

a bird sits in his cage

_____

is the store open

_____

those animals are so cute

_____

hurry up and help the lizard get home

_____

what animals are in the windows

_____

This little lizard got on the roof. Help him find his way through the maze and back inside to his friends. What type of sentence would you use to tell someone that a lizard escaped?

151

A Great Day

A journal or diary is a good place to write your thoughts.

When was the best day you remember? What happened that day? Where did it happen? Who was there? How did the events of that day make you feel? Why? Write about it on this journal page.

_____

_____

_____

_____

_____

_____

_____

_____

_____

_____

_____

Draw a picture of what happened that day.

Thank You!

Pretend you received a great birthday gift. Fill in the blanks of this thank-you note.

Dear _____,

Thank you so much for the _____.
When I opened the package I was
_____ and _____.
I have always wanted to _____.
And now that I have _____, I
can _____. I am looking forward
to seeing you _____. Until then,
let's talk _____. Maybe I can
even send you a picture of _____
_____.

Write and send your own thank-you note!

Sincerely,

_____

Find and circle **8** objects in this Hidden Pictures® scene. What do they all have in common?

fan fork fried egg frog flag feather frying pan fish

Summer Nights

On summer nights when soft winds sigh,
And countless stars caress the sky,
I leave my window open wide
And listen to the world outside:

The crooning crickets, lowing cows,
The creaking of the cedar boughs,
The croaking frogs, the whippoorwills,
Coyotes yipping in the hills.

Their voices linger on the breeze,
Familiar sounds that soothe and ease.
On summer nights, I close my eyes,
Immersed in nature's lullabies.

Your Turn to Rhyme

As you read the poem "Summer Nights," pay attention to the rhyming pattern. Every pair of lines ends with words that rhyme.

Write your own rhyming poem about one of the topics in the theme box. Or you can come up with your own topic.

A rhyming couplet is two lines with last words that rhyme.

Halloween	Summer	Pets	Outer Space
Winter	My Best Day	School	Sports

_____

_____

_____

_____

_____

_____

_____

_____

_____

_____

Pine Tree Gloves

Gloved branches hang low.
Pine fingers shimmer with snow,
Waving as wind blows.

Reading: Haiku

Haiku for You

Read the haiku "Pine Tree Gloves" on page 158. Haiku is a form of poetry that does not have to rhyme, but uses syllables to create a rhythm. The first line has 5 syllables, the second line has 7 syllables, and the third line has 5 syllables again.

Haiku poems are usually about nature.

Try your own haiku here. Count the beats of each word to add up the syllables.

_____

_____

(5-syllable line)

_____

_____

(7-syllable line)

_____

_____

(5-syllable line)

In My Opinion . . .

A review gives your opinion about something.

Write a review of a book or movie you know well. In the first sentence, state the name of the book or movie and explain whether you liked it or not. In the second sentence, describe the things you did or did not like and explain why. In the third sentence, tell whether you think other people would like the book or movie and explain why.

_____

_____

_____

_____

_____

_____

_____

_____

_____

_____

Draw a picture of your favorite part of the book or movie.

A Comic Caper

Find and circle **10** objects in this Hidden Pictures® comic.

Write and draw a comic in these panels about one of the topics in the theme box. Or you can come up with your own topic.

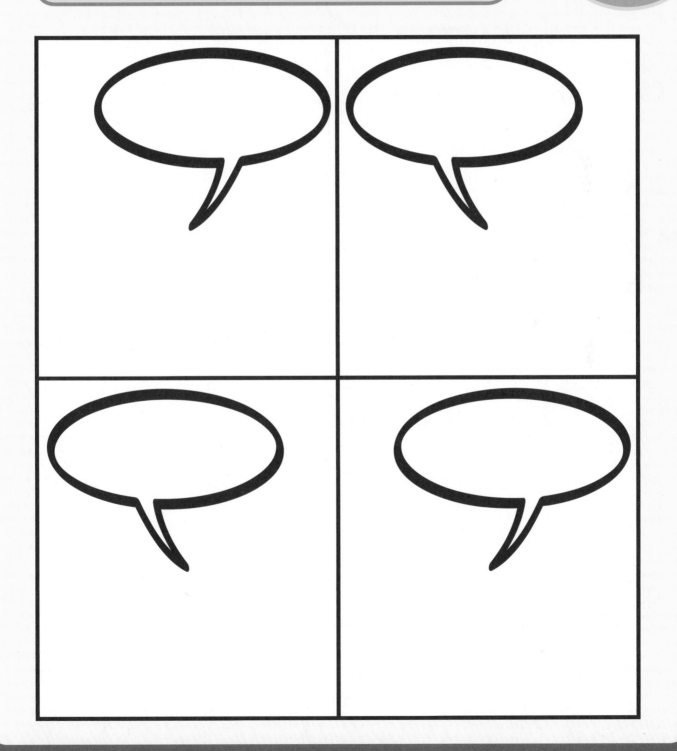

Robots   Animals   Teachers
Superheroes   Kings and Queens   Bugs

This Really Happened

Ask a family member to tell you about something funny that happened to him or her in real life. Write about the funny story here. We'll help you start.

Something funny happened to my

_____. His/Her name is _____.

One time, _____

_____

_____

_____

_____

_____

_____

_____

_____

_____

_____

_____

_____

_____

Could This Happen?

Write a fiction story. We'll help you start.

Once there was a kid named
_____ who lived in _____.
Last summer, this kid rode a rocket ship into
outer space. This is what happened next.

_____

_____

_____

_____

_____

_____

_____

_____

_____

_____

Two by Two

Count by 2's to fill in the missing numbers. Then, each pair of socks has another pair that matches it exactly. Can you find all 10 pairs?

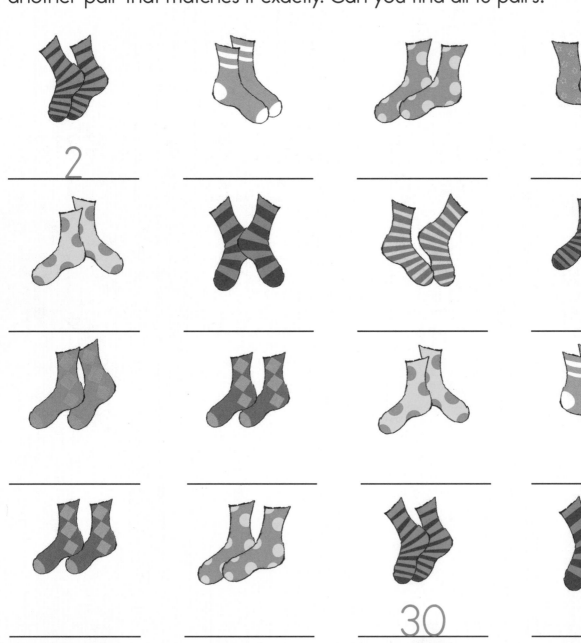

2

16

30

Fun with Fives

Can you find 5 sets of 5 things in this scene?

Fritz drew a maze with 5 sides. Help him get out by following the path that counts by 5's.

Bunches of Ten

How many balloons did Bryce get in all?

Bryce got bunches of balloons for his birthday. Count the bunches by 10's up to 100. We did the first one to get you started.

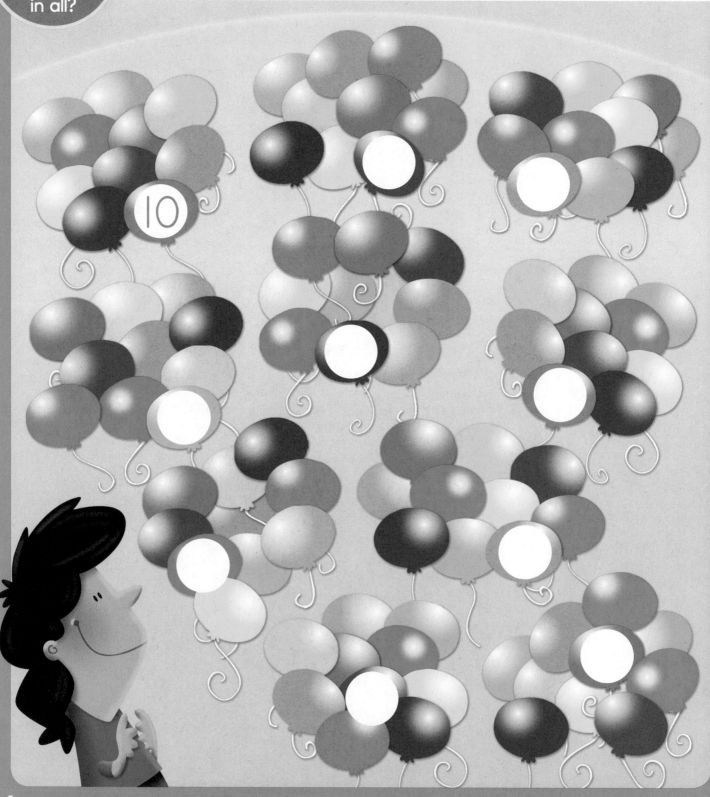

Counting: Skip Count by Tens

Hundreds of Seeds

Try to say this tongue twister seven times: *Shelby saved seven squishy squash seeds.*

Each seed packet has 100 seeds in it. Fill in the blank under each packet to count by 100's up to 1,000. We did the first one to get you started.

PUMPKIN
100 SEEDS INSIDE!

100

BROCCOLI
100 SEEDS INSIDE!

TOMATO
100 SEEDS INSIDE!

SQUASH
100 SEEDS INSIDE!

PEPPER
100 SEEDS INSIDE!

CUCUMBER
100 SEEDS INSIDE!

CARROT
100 SEEDS INSIDE!

LETTUCE
100 SEEDS INSIDE!

EGGPLANT
100 SEEDS INSIDE!

CELERY
100 SEEDS INSIDE!

Happy Hundredth!

Counting: Skip Count by Tens

Snapper is turning 100 today. Connect the dots, counting by 10's, to see what gift he's getting.

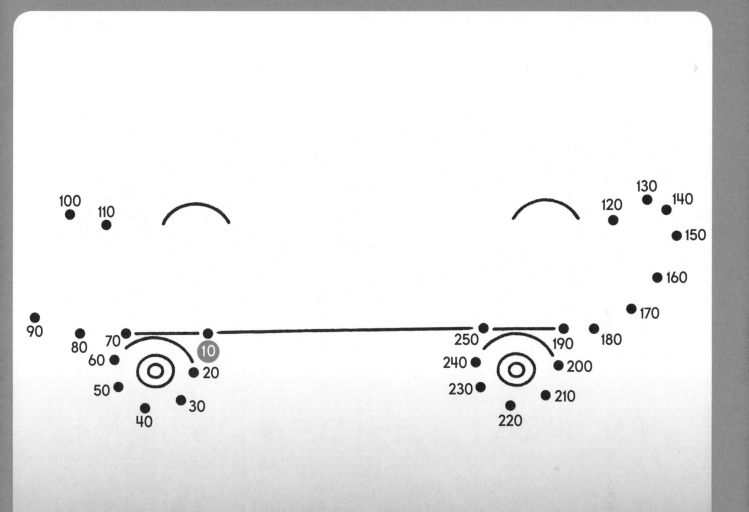

Find and circle **10** objects in the Hidden Pictures® puzzle on the opposite page.

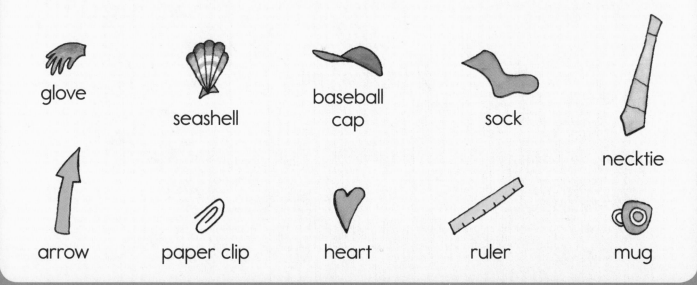

glove

seashell

baseball cap

sock

necktie

arrow

paper clip

heart

ruler

mug

Comparing Numbers

Add the symbol < (less than), > (greater than), or = (equal to) to complete the equations. We filled in the first three to get you started.

The arrow of each symbol always points to the smaller number.

121 < 221   745 > 234   111 = 111

174 ◯ 375   484 ◯ 448   744 ◯ 477

738 ◯ 742   390 ◯ 309   525 ◯ 225

110 ◯ 910   335 ◯ 335   547 ◯ 457

999 ◯ 998   345 ◯ 453   632 ◯ 326

882 ◯ 832   212 ◯ 214   423 ◯ 523

125 ◯ 125   246 ◯ 642   830 ◯ 803

How could drawing a picture of the number pairs help you?

Purr-fect Numbers

Cross out all the even numbers. Then write the letters below the odd numbers in order in the spaces beneath the riddle.

A number ending in 1, 3, 5, 7, or 9 is an odd number.

22	1	6	77	25	84
S	T	O	H	E	P
81	18	63	2	96	17
Y	R	A	E	I	L
75	99	88	9	12	61
L	H	Y	A	G	V
36	62	33	76	47	15
T	R	E	P	N	I
14	79	44	43	28	67
M	N	V	E	Y	L
35	86	41	59	30	7
I	B	V	E	Q	S

Why are cats good at video games?

___ ___ ___ ___ ___   ___ ___ ___

___ ___ ___ ___ ___   ___ ___ ___ ___

___ ___ ___ ___ .

Amusing Numbers

Operations: Ten and Twenty Facts

Can you find at least 20 differences between these pictures?

Can you think of three more addition facts that add up to 20?

7 + ____
13 + ____

0 + ____
20 + ____

3 + ____
17 + ____

20

1 + ____
19 + ____

4 + ____
16 + ____

2 + ____
18 + ____

5 + ____
15 + ____

6 + ____
14 + ____

Pizza Fact Families

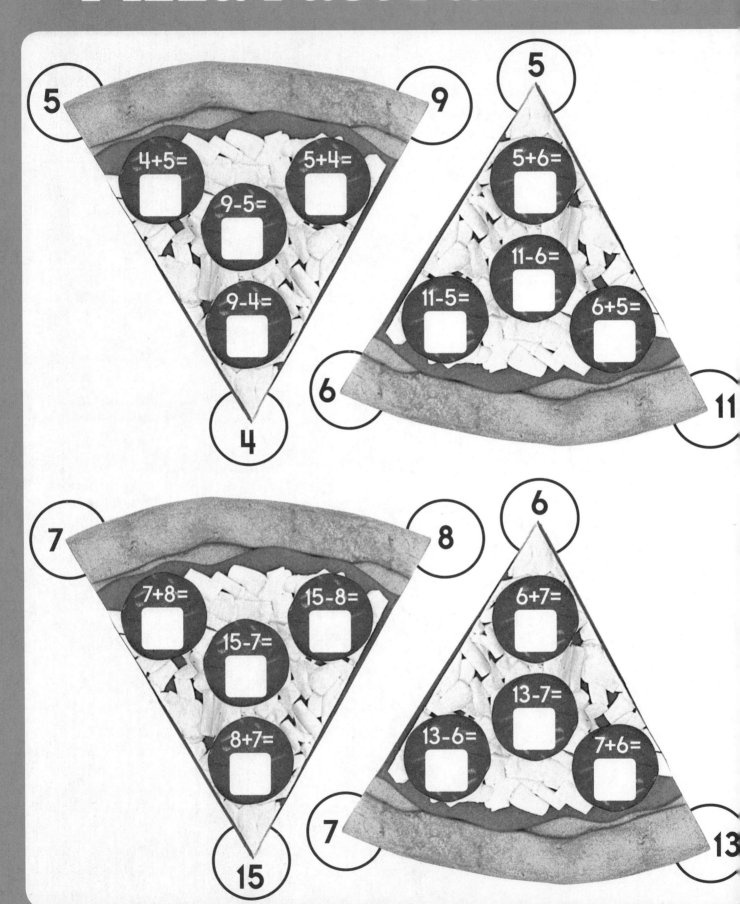

5 · 9 · 4

4+5=

5+4=

9-5=

9-4=

5 · 6 · 11

5+6=

11-6=

11-5=

6+5=

7 · 8 · 15

7+8=

15-8=

15-7=

8+7=

6 · 7 · 13

6+7=

13-7=

13-6=

7+6=

Fill in the blanks to complete the addition and subtraction families.

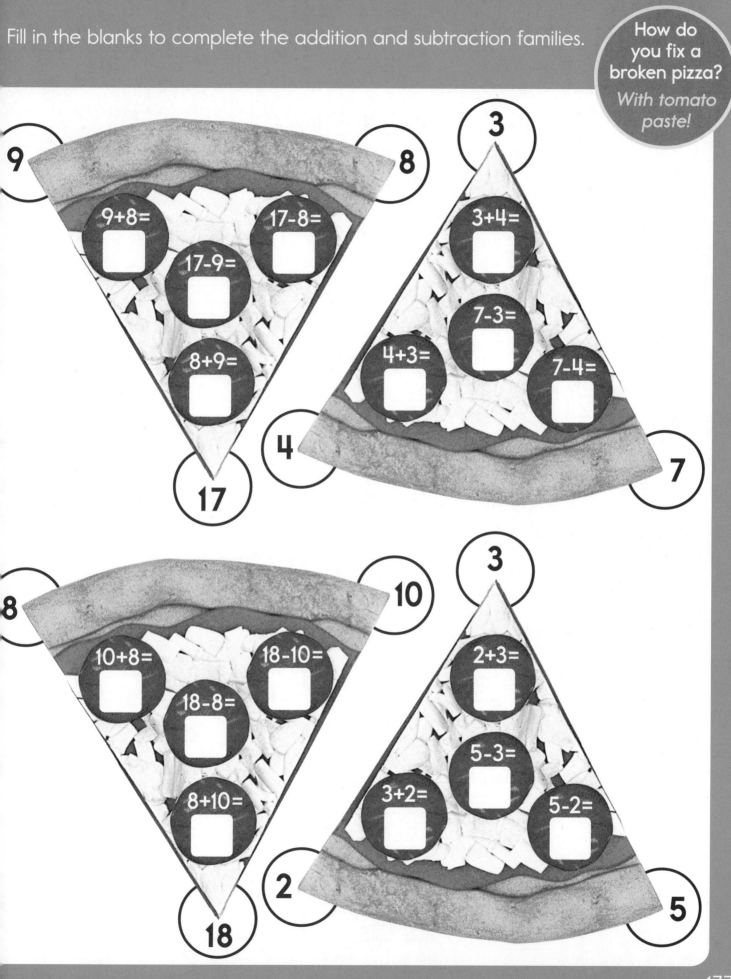

9

8

3

9+8=

17-8=

17-9=

3+4=

8+9=

7-3=

4+3=

7-4=

17

4

7

8

10

3

10+8=

18-10=

18-8=

2+3=

8+10=

5-3=

3+2=

5-2=

18

2

5

177

Place Value

tens	ones
2	5

The **2** tells us there are **2** tens. The **5** tells us there are **5** ones.

 = _20_ + _5_ = _25_

 Write the number of pickles for each example. We did the first to get you started.

= _70_ + _1_ = _71_

 = ___ + ___ = ___

 = ___ + ___ = ___

 = ___ + ___ = ___

 = ___ + ___ = ___

Circle the ones in these numbers:

53   6   17   20

Circle the tens in these numbers:

40   78   23   65

Write the number of tens and ones for each number below:

	tens	ones
49	_____	_____
76	_____	_____
39	_____	_____
92	_____	_____

Knock, knock.
Who's there?
Pickle.
Pickle who?
Pickle little flower to give to your mother.

Place Value

A three-digit number is made up of hundreds, tens, and ones.

hundreds	tens	ones
6	3	4

The **6** tells us there are **6** hundreds. The **3** tells us there are **3** tens. The **4** tells us there are **4** ones.

$$= \underline{600} + \underline{30} + \underline{4} = \underline{634}$$

Write the number of pickles for each example. We did the first to get you started.

$$= \underline{400} + \underline{50} + \underline{3} = \underline{453}$$

$$= \underline{} + \underline{} + \underline{} = \underline{}$$

$$= \underline{} + \underline{} + \underline{} = \underline{}$$

$$= \underline{} + \underline{} + \underline{} = \underline{}$$

Circle the ones in these numbers:

201   57   982   159

Circle the tens in these numbers:

435   973   624   318

Circle the hundreds in these numbers:

105   792   367   503

Draw a line to match each number to the digits in each place value.

354   5 hundreds, 0 tens, 3 ones

503   8 hundreds, 3 tens, 6 ones

29   3 hundreds, 5 tens, 4 ones

836   0 hundreds, 2 tens, 9 ones

Why did the pickle go to the doctor?

He was feeling dill.

The Race Is On

These three runners' race numbers got mixed up. Use the clues to figure out which number belongs to which runner. Then find and circle **8** objects in this Hidden Pictures® puzzle.

48 **74** **81**

The runner in the lead has a race number with 8 tens and 1 one.

The runner with brown hair has a race number with 4 tens and 8 ones.

The runner wearing teal has a race number with a 4 in the ones place.

candle · piece of popcorn · fish · slice of pie · teapot · banana · fork · book

Number Flags

What did the flag say to the math teacher? *Nothing, it just waved.*

Draw a line to match each number to its word version.

764 ○ ○ seventy-six

245 ○ ○ three hundred twenty-seven

536 ○ ○ twenty-five

76 ○ ○ two hundred forty-five

327 ○ ○ three hundred sixty-three

25 ○ ○ seven hundred sixty-four

363 ○ ○ five hundred thirty-six

Sky High

Write these numbers in the windows of the building in order from greatest to least. Write the highest number on the top. Write the lowest number on the bottom. We did one to get you started.

605   158   424   ~~720~~   46   535

Find and circle **12** objects in this Hidden Pictures® puzzle.

artist's brush

bowl

button

mug

ruler

tennis ball

Write these numbers in the windows of the building in order from least to greatest. Write the lowest number on the bottom. Write the highest number on the top. We did one to get you started.

777   299   ~~100~~   684   890   301

I   0   0

candle   pencil   domino   needle   spoon   toothbrush

Addition Mission

START

13+7=☐

☐+10=31

10+18=☐

30+2=☐

11+11=☐

32+☐=64   ☐+81=92

23+10=☐

44+13=☐

18+☐=49   24+25=☐

56+☐=76

31+13=☐   1+☐=29

2+☐=29

10+22=☐

6+☐=39   ☐+63=7☐

12+14=☐

13+☐=45

4+☐=29

☐+5=28   22+2=☐

+34=56

31+3=☐

50+29=☐

33+☐=57

24+53=☐

26+13=☐

31+53=☐

41+16=☐

44+44=☐

☐+76=89

15+☐=37

15+51=☐

10+10=☐

37+☐=39

☐+22=57

Astronaut Andrew and his trusty sidekick Zonks are lost in space. You can help! Write the missing numbers to complete each problem. Then follow the numbers you wrote in order from **20** to **40** to help them get home.

92+4=☐
28+☐=79
14+☐=28
☐+32=59
13+16=☐
☐+=32
10+☐=40
32+☐=85
☐+30=65
12+☐=48
38+21=☐
☐+15=99
21+☐=29
22+12=☐
☐+7=68
22+15=☐
14+41=☐
☐+21=59
81+18=☐
80+13=☐
22+☐=44
30+☐=53
15+82=☐
10+☐=49
30+☐
10+30=☐
☐+7=39
20+18=☐
36+☐=58
51+31=☐
26+☐=37
32+7=☐
10+☐=66
33+24=☐
52+13=☐
21+12=☐

FINISH

187

Add Them Up!

Solve these addition problems. We did the first one to get you started.

23 + 34 **57**	35 + 61	33 + 12	42 + 36
14 + 15	25 + 53	344 +535	665 +324
645 +133	753 +120	724 +203	129 +160

Color the scene below. How many animals can you count? How many people can you count? How many animals and people are there all together?

Solve these addition problems.

62 + 35 = [ ]

76 + 22 = [ ]

50 + 23 = [ ]

81 + 10 = [ ]

92 + 5 = [ ]

566 + 103 = [ ]

303 + 84 = [ ]

537 + 212 = [ ]

456 + 333 = [ ]

828 + 30 = [ ]

What strategy did you use to solve these problems? Can you think of another way to solve them?

ONE WAY

ICE CREAM

Two-Digit Addition

You can use place values to help add numbers using **regrouping**. Look at this example:

$$37$$
$$+\ 29$$
$$\boxed{}$$

When you add the numbers in the ones value column, you get **16**. But you can't have more than **9** in the ones value.

$$37$$
$$+\ 29$$
$$\boxed{6}$$

So you can regroup the **16** into **1 tens value and 6 ones value**.

$$37$$
$$+\ 29$$
$$\boxed{66}$$

Now that you've traded **10** ones for **1** ten, you can add that **1** up with the other numbers in the tens column.

· ·

You can look at this same problem using pickles.

You get:

Now you have:

· ·

Write these as numbers. (Remember, every time you end up with more than **9** ones, trade **10** ones for **1** ten and leave the ones that remain.)

7 tens, 12 ones = $\boxed{}$ 6 tens, 17 ones = $\boxed{}$

2 tens, 15 ones = $\boxed{}$ 5 tens, 18 ones = $\boxed{}$

Double Digits

When you make a 10, you have to trade the 10 ones for 1 ten. You can write it as a 1 above the tens column.

Add these numbers. Remember to trade **10** ones for **1** ten when you have more than **9** ones. We did the first one to get you started.

How could adding by place value help you solve each problem?

```
  1
  32        45        59
+ 29      + 37      + 18
┌──┐      ┌──┐      ┌──┐
│61│      │  │      │  │
└──┘      └──┘      └──┘
```

```
  72        43        47
+ 19      + 49      + 27
┌──┐      ┌──┐      ┌──┐
│  │      │  │      │  │
└──┘      └──┘      └──┘
```

16 + 26 = ☐   53 + 17 = ☐

19 + 19 = ☐   55 + 28 = ☐

27 + 36 = ☐   15 + 7 = ☐

How do you make a squid laugh?

With ten-tickles

Three-Digit Addition

Now let's try regrouping with triple-digit numbers. Look at this example:

$$273 + 559 = \square$$

When you add the numbers in the ones value column, you get **12**. But you can't have more than **9** in the ones value. So you can regroup the **12** into **1 tens value and 2 ones value.**

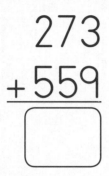

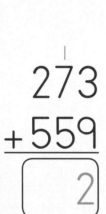

Now that you've traded **10** ones for **1** ten and moved it over to the tens column, you can add that **1** up with the other numbers in the tens column to get **13**. But you can't have more than **9** in the tens value. So you can regroup the **13** into **1 hundreds value and 3 tens value.**

Now you can add the numbers in the hundreds column.

$$273 + 559 = 32$$

$$273 + 559 = 832$$

....

Write these as numbers. (Remember, every time you end up with more than **9** ones, trade **10** ones for **1** ten and leave the ones that remain. And every time you end up with more than **9** tens, trade **10** tens for **1** hundred and leave the tens that remain.)

3 hundreds, 17 tens, 2 ones = $\square$

6 hundreds, 10 tens, 14 ones = $\square$

5 hundreds, 12 tens, 2 ones = $\square$

7 hundreds, 18 tens, 15 ones = $\square$

Triple Digits

What strategy did you use to solve these problems? How do you remember that you traded 10 ones for 1 ten or 10 tens for 1 hundred?

Add these numbers. Remember to trade **10** ones for **1** ten when you have more than **9** ones, and to trade **10** tens for **1** hundred when you have more than **9** tens. We did the first one to get you started.

$$
\begin{array}{r} 117 \\ +\ 38 \\ \hline \boxed{155} \end{array}
\qquad
\begin{array}{r} 385 \\ +\ 38 \\ \hline \boxed{} \end{array}
\qquad
\begin{array}{r} 456 \\ +254 \\ \hline \boxed{} \end{array}
$$

$$
\begin{array}{r} 448 \\ +289 \\ \hline \boxed{} \end{array}
\qquad
\begin{array}{r} 393 \\ +362 \\ \hline \boxed{} \end{array}
\qquad
\begin{array}{r} 747 \\ +226 \\ \hline \boxed{} \end{array}
$$

$709 + 123 = \boxed{}$ $\qquad$ $106 + 44 = \boxed{}$

$327 + 482 = \boxed{}$ $\qquad$ $199 + 11 = \boxed{}$

$394 + 367 = \boxed{}$ $\qquad$ $303 + 217 = \boxed{}$

Try to say this tongue twister seven times, fast!

Didi goes gaga over digits.

Turtle Crossing

```
  24        39        56        33        24
+ 48      + 15      + 27      + 11      + 13
┌──────┐  ┌────┐    ┌────┐    ┌────┐    ┌────┐
│  72  │  │    │    │    │    │    │    │    │
│  A   │  └────┘    └────┘    └────┘    └────┘
└──────┘
```

```
  72        41        39        52        59
+ 11      + 21      + 28      + 47      + 19
┌────┐    ┌────┐    ┌────┐    ┌────┐    ┌────┐
│    │    │    │    │    │    │    │    │    │
└────┘    └────┘    └────┘    └────┘    └────┘
```

28 + 13 = ☐   21 + 46 = ☐

29 + 27 = ☐   52 + 15 = ☐

72 + 9 = ☐   83 + 12 = ☐

60 + 23 = ☐   28 + 16 = ☐

47 + 34 = ☐

Solve each problem on page 194. Use the code to write the matching letter in the bottom half of the blank. When you're done, write the letters in order from left to right and top to bottom in the boxes below. We did the first one to get you started.

A = 72   H = 95   O = 83

B = 54   I = 78   P = 56

E = 67   L = 41   R = 81

           M = 99   T = 37

           N = 62   U = 44

What was the turtle doing on the highway?

A							

Subtraction Action

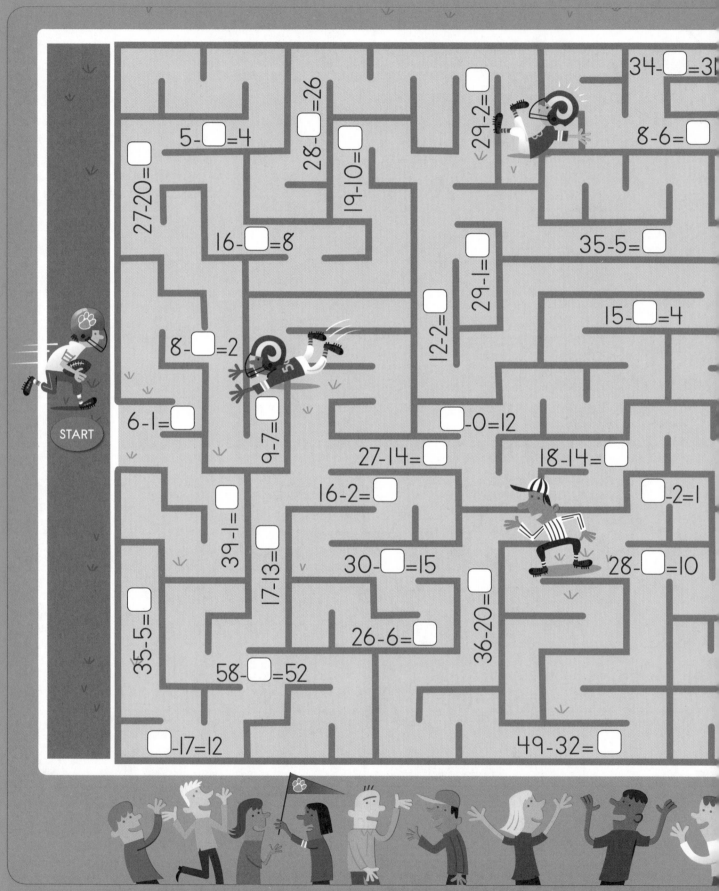

START

$27-20=\boxed{}$

$5-\boxed{}=4$

$28-\boxed{}=26$

$19-10=\boxed{}$

$16-\boxed{}=8$

$29-2=\boxed{}$

$34-\boxed{}=3\boxed{}$

$8-6=\boxed{}$

$35-5=\boxed{}$

$29-1=\boxed{}$

$12-2=\boxed{}$

$15-\boxed{}=4$

$8-\boxed{}=2$

$6-1=\boxed{}$

$9-7=\boxed{}$

$\boxed{}-0=12$

$27-14=\boxed{}$

$18-14=\boxed{}$

$16-2=\boxed{}$

$\boxed{}-2=1$

$39-1=\boxed{}$

$17-13=\boxed{}$

$30-\boxed{}=15$

$28-\boxed{}=10$

$35-5=\boxed{}$

$26-6=\boxed{}$

$36-20=\boxed{}$

$58-\boxed{}=52$

$\boxed{}-17=12$

$49-32=\boxed{}$

Otto just caught the return kick. Now he's ready to run all the way to the end zone. You can help! Write the missing numbers to complete each problem. Then follow the numbers you wrote in order from **5** to **25** to score a touchdown.

50-☐=30

43-10=☐

13-10=☐

26-4=☐

☐-8=11

25-12=☐

18-12=☐

38-☐=12

☐-12=12

27-0=☐

4-3=☐

36-☐=13

7-5=☐

28-3=☐

FINISH

24-2=☐

☐-4=13

36-3=☐

9-6=☐

21-0=☐

29-10=☐

33-3=☐

42-☐=31

28-☐=8

What's the Difference?

Solve these subtraction problems. We did the first one to get you started.

77	95	33	48
− 34	− 61	− 12	− 36
43	☐	☐	☐

19	85	69	76
− 12	− 53	− 35	− 22
☐	☐	☐	☐

What strategy did you use to solve these problems? Can you think of another way to solve them?

	81	98	28
	− 20	− 5	− 11
	☐	☐	☐

The answers to subtraction problems are called **differences.** Can you find **16** differences between the two pictures below the subtraction problems?

Solve these subtraction problems.

78 – 35 = ☐   86 – 45 = ☐

86 – 32 = ☐   39 – 14 = ☐

45 – 33 = ☐   57 – 22 = ☐

78 – 25 = ☐   46 – 33 = ☐

72 – 60 = ☐   82 – 10 = ☐

29 – 18 = ☐   65 – 34 = ☐

Let's Regroup

You can use place values to help subtract numbers using **regrouping**. Look at this example:

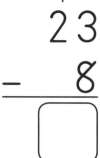

When you try to subtract the numbers in the ones value column, it doesn't work. You can't take **8** from **3**. So you have to "borrow" a ten from the tens column.

So you can regroup the ones into **1 tens value and 3 ones value**, or 13.

Now that you've traded **1** ten for **10** ones and moved them over to the ones column, you can subtract the numbers in the ones column.

● ●

You can look at this same problem using pickles.

You can't take **8** from **3** so you'll need to "open" a jar of pickles to get more loose pickles to trade to the ones column.

Now you can subtract to get:

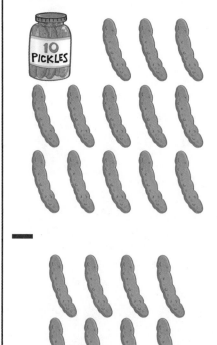

Double Digits

When regrouping, put the number you are moving above the place value where it will go.

Subtract these numbers. Remember to borrow **1** ten and trade it for **10** ones whenever you need more ones. We did the first one to get you started.

$$\begin{array}{r} \overset{1}{\cancel{2}}5 \\ -\ \ 6 \\ \hline \boxed{19} \end{array} \qquad \begin{array}{r} 90 \\ -\ \ 7 \\ \hline \boxed{} \end{array} \qquad \begin{array}{r} 85 \\ -\ \ 8 \\ \hline \boxed{} \end{array} \qquad \begin{array}{r} 64 \\ -\ 17 \\ \hline \boxed{} \end{array}$$

$$\begin{array}{r} 51 \\ -\ 33 \\ \hline \boxed{} \end{array} \qquad \begin{array}{r} 28 \\ -\ 19 \\ \hline \boxed{} \end{array} \qquad \begin{array}{r} 64 \\ -\ 49 \\ \hline \boxed{} \end{array} \qquad \begin{array}{r} 55 \\ -\ 28 \\ \hline \boxed{} \end{array}$$

$$\begin{array}{r} 71 \\ -\ 36 \\ \hline \boxed{} \end{array} \qquad \begin{array}{r} 16 \\ -\ \ 9 \\ \hline \boxed{} \end{array} \qquad \begin{array}{r} 24 \\ -\ 16 \\ \hline \boxed{} \end{array} \qquad \begin{array}{r} 45 \\ -\ 27 \\ \hline \boxed{} \end{array}$$

What did the plus sign say to the minus sign?

"You are so negative!"

Let's Regroup

Now let's try regrouping with triple-digit numbers. Look at this example:

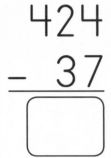

When you try to subtract the numbers in the ones value column, it doesn't work. You can't take **7** from **4**. So, you have to "borrow" a ten from the tens column. You can regroup the ones into **1 tens value and 4 ones value**, or **14**.

Now that you've traded **1** ten for **10** ones and moved them over to the ones column, you can subtract the ones values.

Next, try to subtract the numbers in the tens column. Again, it doesn't work. You can't take **3** from **1**. You will need to borrow again, this time from the hundreds column.

Now you can finish subtracting.

See if you can say this tongue twister five times, fast!

Silly subtraction surprises Shelby.

Triple Digits

When regrouping, put the number you are moving above the place value where it will go.

Subtract these numbers. Remember to borrow from the tens place when you need more ones, and to borrow from the hundreds place when you need more tens. We did the first one to get you started.

$$
\begin{array}{r}
1\,\overset{8}{\cancel{9}}\,{}^{1}7 \\
-38 \\
\hline
159
\end{array}
$$

$$
\begin{array}{r}
385 \\
-156 \\
\hline
\boxed{}
\end{array}
$$

$$
\begin{array}{r}
456 \\
-208 \\
\hline
\boxed{}
\end{array}
$$

$$
\begin{array}{r}
448 \\
-219 \\
\hline
\boxed{}
\end{array}
$$

$$
\begin{array}{r}
393 \\
-366 \\
\hline
\boxed{}
\end{array}
$$

$$
\begin{array}{r}
747 \\
-266 \\
\hline
\boxed{}
\end{array}
$$

$$
\begin{array}{r}
327 \\
-182 \\
\hline
\boxed{}
\end{array}
$$

$$
\begin{array}{r}
364 \\
-172 \\
\hline
\boxed{}
\end{array}
$$

$$
\begin{array}{r}
159 \\
-61 \\
\hline
\boxed{}
\end{array}
$$

$$
\begin{array}{r}
307 \\
-13 \\
\hline
\boxed{}
\end{array}
$$

$$
\begin{array}{r}
253 \\
-166 \\
\hline
\boxed{}
\end{array}
$$

$$
\begin{array}{r}
426 \\
-188 \\
\hline
\boxed{}
\end{array}
$$

What do you call a soccer player who loves arithmetic?

A mathlete

The Art of Subtraction

$$68 - 31 = \boxed{37}$$

$$83 - 14 = \boxed{}$$

$$48 - 27 = \boxed{}$$

$$57 - 36 = \boxed{}$$

$$96 - 48 = \boxed{}$$

$$74 - 55 = \boxed{}$$

$$49 - 15 = \boxed{}$$

$$51 - 25 = \boxed{}$$

$$87 - 39 = \boxed{}$$

$$90 - 38 = \boxed{}$$

Solve each problem on page 204. Use the code to write the matching letter in the bottom half of the blank. When you're done, write the letters in order from left to right and top to bottom in the boxes below. We did the first one to get you started.

A = 34   N = 48

E = 21   P = 19

G = 37   R = 69

I = 26   T = 52

What is green and smells like blue paint?

G				

Marble Addition

Each group has 3 marbles. How many marbles are there all together? You can add them:

$$3 + 3 + 3 + 3 = 12$$

4 rows with 3 marbles each

Finish the repeated addition equations. Then write how many rows and how many marbles in each row there are in total.

$$2 + \underline{} + \underline{} + \underline{} = \underline{}$$

$\underline{}$ rows with $\underline{}$ marbles each

$$4 + \underline{} + \underline{} = \underline{}$$

$\underline{}$ rows with $\underline{}$ marbles each

5 + ___ + ___ = ___

___ rows with ___ marbles each

6 + ___ + ___ = ___

___ rows with ___ marbles each

8 + ___ + ___ = ___

___ rows with ___ marbles each

Score Big

It's the end of the first half in the big game. Solve the word problems below to figure out which team is winning. We did the first one to get you started.

Kayla Kangaroo scored six 2-point shots. How many points did she get?

$$\underline{2} + \underline{2} + \underline{2} + \underline{2} + \underline{2} + \underline{2} = \underline{12}$$

Kenny Kangaroo scored seven 3-point shots. How many points did he get?

$$\underline{} + \underline{} + \underline{} + \underline{} + \underline{} + \underline{} + \underline{} = \underline{}$$

George Giraffe scored eight 1-point foul shots. How many points did he get?

$$\underline{} + \underline{} + \underline{} + \underline{} + \underline{} + \underline{} + \underline{} + \underline{} = \underline{}$$

Ginny Giraffe scored five 2-point shots and three 3-point shots. How many points did she get?

$$\underline{} + \underline{} + \underline{} + \underline{} + \underline{} = \underline{}$$

$$\underline{} + \underline{} + \underline{} = \underline{}$$

Which team is in the lead?   ○ Kangaroos   ○ Giraffes

Find and circle **5** objects in this Hidden Pictures® puzzle. What do they have in common?

test tube

eye dropper

beaker

magnet

goggles

Tracing Fun!

Trace each of these shapes. Write the correct name from the word bank under each shape.

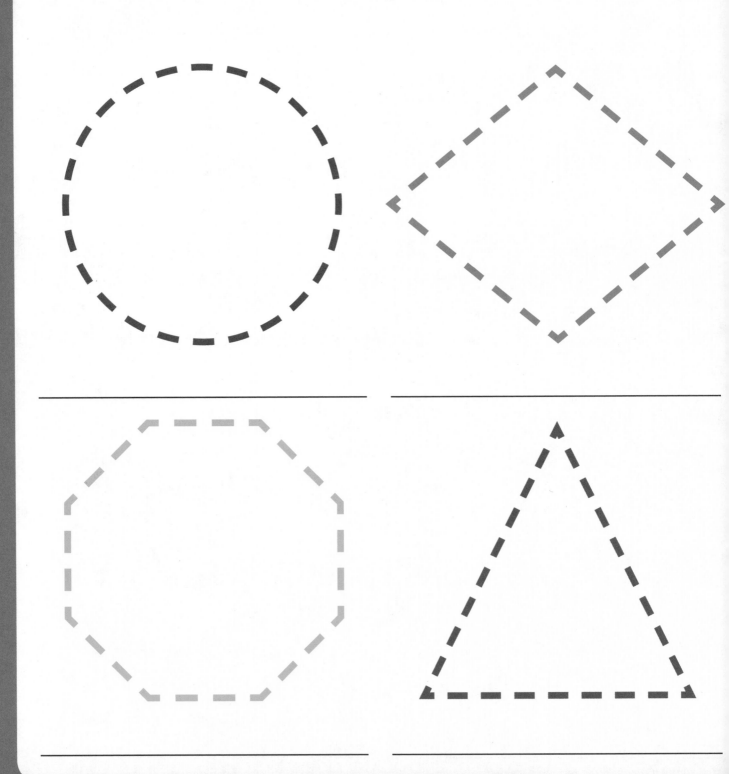

Geometry: Two-Dimensional Shapes

Knock, knock.
Who's there?
Brent.
Brent who?
Brent out of shape!

circle   octagon   oval   pentagon
rectangle   rhombus   square   triangle

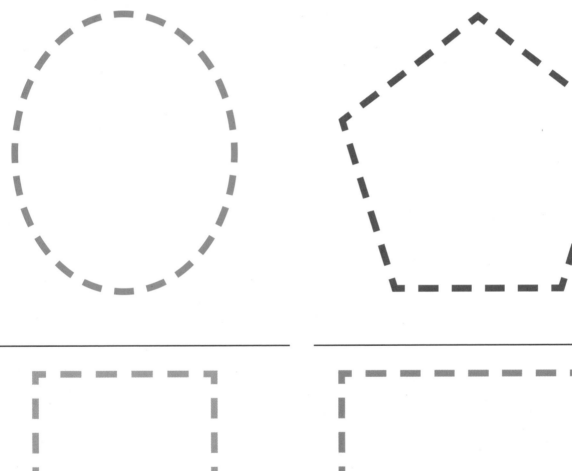

3-D Shapes

Match each 3-dimensional shape to its name.

cone ○ ○

cube ○ ○

cylinder ○ ○

pyramid ○ ○

rectangular prism ○ ○

sphere ○

With a parent's permission, hunt for empty boxes, cardboard tubes, cans, and balls in your home. What 3-D shapes did you find? What can you make with them?

Each of these objects is an example of a 3-D shape. Write the shape name from the word bank under each object. Can you think of other things that have these shapes?

3-dimensional shapes have height, width, and depth.

| cone | cube | cylinder |
| pyramid | rectangular prism | sphere |

_____

_____

Parts of a Whole

Color in one half (½) of each shape. We did the first one to get you started.

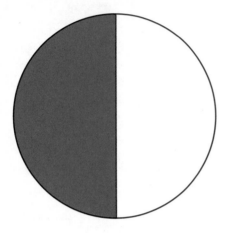

Color in one fourth (¼) of each shape. We did the first one to get you started.

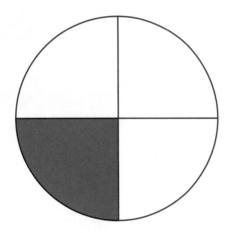
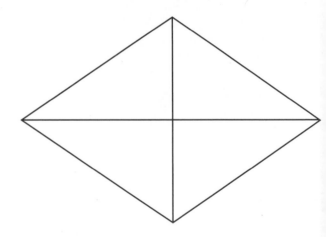

Color in one third (⅓) of each shape. We did the first one to get you started.

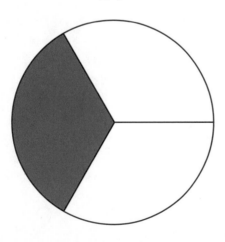
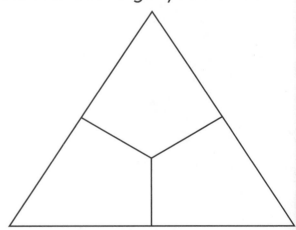

A thing is divided in half when it is cut in two equal parts. It is divided in thirds when it is cut in three equal parts. And it is divided in fourths, or quarters, when it is cut in four equal parts.

Fractions are written with the number of parts above the line, and the total number of parts below the line. So ½ is 1 part out of a total of 2.

If you eat two-thirds of a pie, what do you have?

An angry baker

215

Fraction Fun

Solve these riddles using the letters in the words. Each fraction tells you which letters to use. We filled in the first letter to get you started.

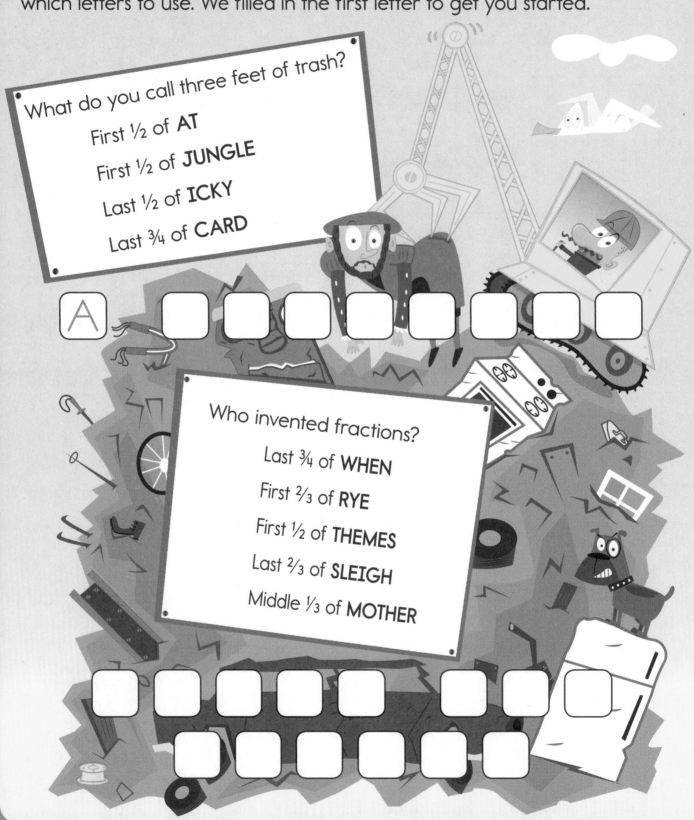

What do you call three feet of trash?

First ½ of **AT**

First ½ of **JUNGLE**

Last ½ of **ICKY**

Last ¾ of **CARD**

A

Who invented fractions?

Last ¾ of **WHEN**

First ⅔ of **RYE**

First ½ of **THEMES**

Last ⅔ of **SLEIGH**

Middle ⅓ of **MOTHER**

How to Measure?

Would you use a ruler or a measuring tape to measure . . .

The length of a classroom?

The height of a book?

The height of a person?

The length of a basketball court?

The width of a piece of paper?

Why did the boy put a ruler
next to his bed?

*Because he wanted to see
how long he slept*

Do You Measure Up?

Stretch out your arms so your body makes a T shape. Ask a friend or parent to use a tape measure to measure from the tips of your fingers on one hand to the tips of your fingers on the other hand. Is your "wingspan" larger or smaller than the wingspan of these birds?

Which bird is closest to your "wingspan" size?

mallard duck
36 inches

☐ larger   ☐ smaller

barn owl
44 inches

☐ larger   ☐ smaller

red-tailed hawk
48 inches

☐ larger   ☐ smaller

great horned owl
55 inches

☐ larger   ☐ smaller

common loon
58 inches

☐ larger   ☐ smaller

blue-footed booby
62 inches

☐ larger   ☐ smaller

turkey vulture
72 inches

☐ larger   ☐ smaller

bald eagle
80 inches

☐ larger   ☐ smaller

My "wingspan" is _____ inches.

Place your foot on a piece of paper and trace around it. Measure the length of your tracing from the heel to the tip of your big toe. Is your "track" longer or shorter than the tracks of these animals?

mountain lion
3 inches

☐ shorter ☐ longer

raccoon
4 inches

☐ shorter ☐ longer

wolverine
5 inches

☐ shorter ☐ longer

sea otter
6 inches

☐ shorter ☐ longer

black bear
8 inches

☐ shorter ☐ longer

grizzly bear
10 inches

☐ shorter ☐ longer

polar bear
12 inches

☐ shorter ☐ longer

My "track" is _____ inches.

219

Your Money's Worth...

Circle the answer for each coin.

I am worth 1¢. I am a:

I am worth 5¢. I am a:

I am worth 10¢. I am a:

I am worth 25¢. I am a:

I am worth 100¢. I am a:

Circle the total for each group of coins and bills.

     = $1.05   87¢ $1.41

     = 28¢   96¢ $1.75

    = $1.38   63¢ $1.23

     = 94¢ $1.23   85¢

Add up the coins in each group. Circle each group that adds up to $1.00

....

When five friends cleaned out their backpacks, they saw that each of them needs just one coin to have a dollar. What coin does each one need?

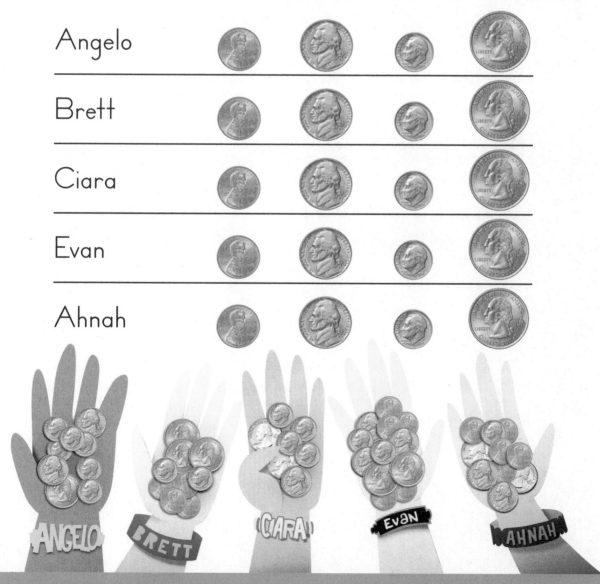

Toys for Twins

Nate and Jada want to get presents for their twin brothers. They each have $6.00 to spend.

If Nate buys the dinosaur puzzle and the paint set, how much will that cost?

Dinosaur puzzle		$_____
Paint set	+	$_____
Total		$_____

How much change will he get back?

Nate has		$____6.00____
Nate spends	−	$_____
Nate gets back		$_____

If Jada buys the magic kit and the dump truck, how much will that cost?

Magic kit		$_____
Dump truck	+	$_____
Total		$_____

How much change will she get back?

Jada has		$____6.00____
Jada spends	−	$_____
Jada gets back		$_____

Around the Clock

The numbers **1** through **12** on a clock mark every **5** minutes. Count by **5**'s around the clock up to **60** minutes (1 hour). We did the first one to get you started.

What has two hands but doesn't clap?
A clock

Write the time shown on each clock.

Look at each clock. What time will it be in 10 minutes? What time was it 2 hours ago?

_____

_____

_____

Time Codes

What do workers do in a clock factory?

___ ___ ___ ___   ___ ___ ___ ___ ___
6:15 1:30 3:00 10:30   11:00 1:30 11:30 10:30 9:10

When is a clock nervous?

                                         ,

___ ___ ___ ___   ___ ___ ___   ___ ___ ___
8:30 6:00 10:30 1:00   4:00 6:30 9:10   1:30 6:55 6:55

___ ___ ___ ___ ___   ___ ___
8:30 3:45 3:30 1:00 12:00   3:30 5:05

Write the letters from the clocks onto the correct lines below. Each digital time will match up with one of the clocks. Fill in all the blanks to learn the punchlines to the riddles.

Community Park

Name 3 words or phrases that describe your community.

Name something you can do to help your community.

These neighbors are working together to build a new park in their community. Is this an urban, suburban, or rural community? How can you tell? Find and circle **24** objects in this Hidden Pictures® puzzle.

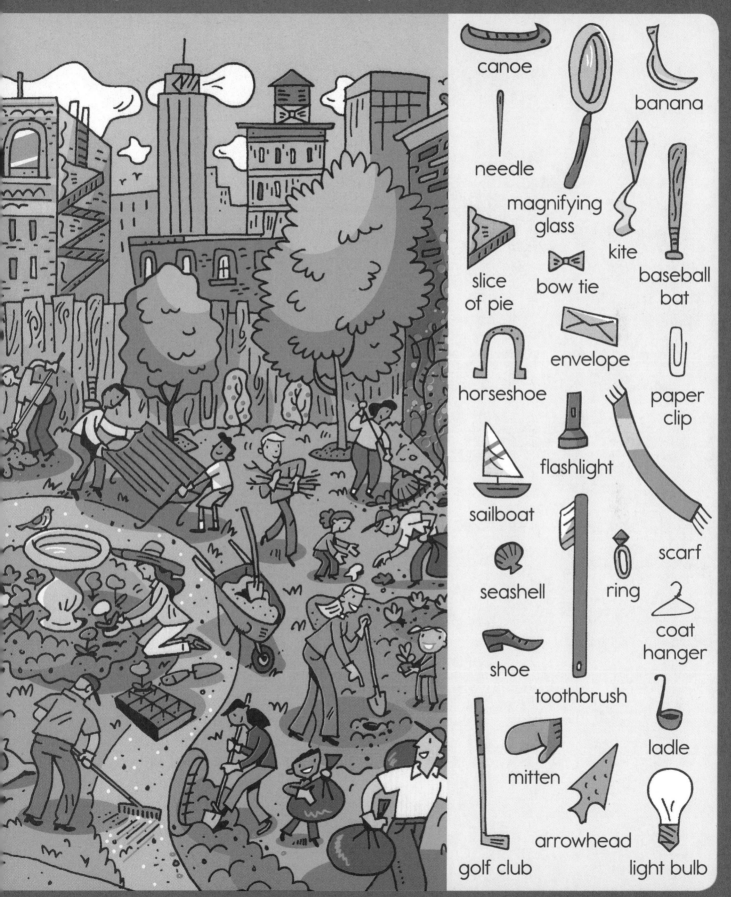

canoe

needle

magnifying glass

slice of pie

bow tie

kite

baseball bat

banana

envelope

horseshoe

flashlight

paper clip

sailboat

scarf

seashell

ring

coat hanger

shoe

toothbrush

ladle

mitten

arrowhead

golf club

light bulb

Job Search

Name 3 jobs you see in your community. What is your dream job?

Find the names of 21 jobs hidden in this word search. To find them, look up, down, across, backward, and diagonally. We found one to get you started. Can you find the rest?

ACTOR
ARTIST
ATHLETE
BANKER
BUILDER
CHEF
DENTIST
DOCTOR
FARMER
FIREFIGHTER
JANITOR
LIBRARIAN
MAYOR
PILOT
POLICE OFFICER
SCIENTIST
SINGER
TEACHER
VETERINARIAN
WAITER
WRITER

```
Y C M G R Q Y L D O C T O R
T S I T N E D I H O O M U M
G S Y S M T S B Q R Q T W F
B S I N G E R R X E Q R F I
T O L I P V A A R C R O U R
D E R T J N B R E I E T T E
J R A E S P U I K F T C S F
L L X C T I W A N F I A I I
C E E H H I T N A O R U T G
W Y V B E E A N B E W O R H
F A R M E R R W E C G L A T
V E T E R I N A R I A N O E
D J J I R O Y A M L C W X R
A T H L E T E L Q O P S D O
B U I L D E R K G P F E H C
A X K C R O T I N A J N C Q
```

Themes of Citizenship

Write or draw an example for each of the 5 themes of citizenship below. You might think of a time that you or someone you know displayed one of these themes.

HONESTY

COMPASSION

RESPECT

RESPONSIBILITY

COURAGE

You can look up each theme in the dictionary, or you might talk with friends or family about what these themes mean to them.

Our United States

This is a map of the United States of America. Use the map to help you answer the questions on page 234.

COMPASS ROSE

A compass rose is a symbol that shows directions on a map.

Map Adventure

Answer these questions. Use the map on pages 232–233 to help.

What state do you live in?

_____

In what state is the Statue of Liberty?

_____

In what state is the Grand Canyon?

_____

Which two states are not part of the contiguous
(connected) USA? _____

Which state is north of Alabama?
      ○ Mississippi   ○ Tennessee   ○ Georgia

Which state is south of Oklahoma?
      ○ Texas   ○ Colorado   ○ Missouri

Which state is east of Pennsylvania?
      ○ New Jersey ○ Ohio   ○ Maryland

Which state is west of Nevada?
      ○ Idaho   ○ California ○ Utah

· ·

Why is Alabama the smartest state?
Because it has four A's and one B

· ·

What did Tennessee?
The same thing that Arkansas

Scrambled States

If you unscramble the letters on the light blue balloons, you can spell HAWAII. Which 9 other states can you spell using each colored group of balloons?

The Great State Search

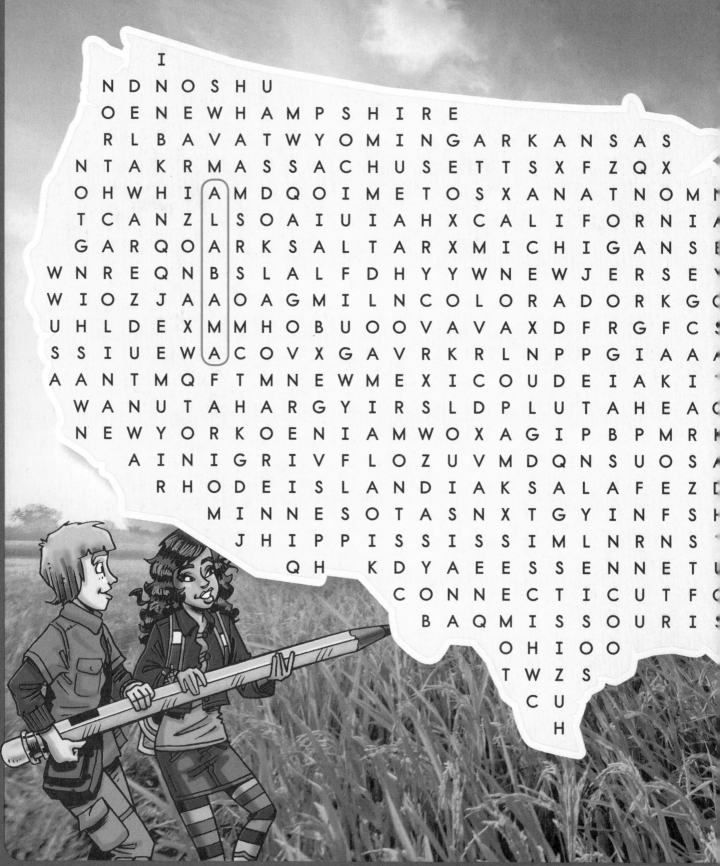

```
        I
    N D N O S H U
    O E N E W H A M P S H I R E
    R L B A V A T W Y O M I N G A R K A N S A S
  N T A K R M A S S A C H U S E T T S X F Z Q X
  O H W H I A M D Q O I M E T O S X A N A T N O M
  T C A N Z L S O A I U I A H X C A L I F O R N I A
  G A R Q O A R K S A L T A R X M I C H I G A N S E
W N R E Q N B S L A L F D H Y Y W N E W J E R S E Y
W I O Z J A A O A G M I L N C O L O R A D O R K G O
U H L D E X M M H O B U O O V A V A X D F R G F C S
S S I U E W A C O V X G A V R K R L N P P G I A A A
A A N T M Q F T M N E W M E X I C O U D E I A K I T
W A N U T A H A R G Y I R S L D P L U T A H E A C
N E W Y O R K O E N I A M W O X A G I P B P M R H
  A I N I G R I V F L O Z U V M D Q N S U O S A
  R H O D E I S L A N D I A K S A L A F E Z D
    M I N N E S O T A S N X T G Y I N F S H
    J H I P P I S S I S S I M L N R N S T
    Q H   K D Y A E E S S E N N E T U
        C O N N E C T I C U T F O
        B A Q M I S S O U R I S
          O H I O O
          T W Z S
          C U H
```

All 50 states are hiding in this USA-shaped puzzle. They are hidden forward, backward, up, down, and diagonally. We circled one to get you started.

ALABAMA	MONTANA
ALASKA	NEBRASKA
ARIZONA	NEVADA
ARKANSAS	NEW HAMPSHIRE
CALIFORNIA	NEW JERSEY
COLORADO	NEW MEXICO
CONNECTICUT	NEW YORK
DELAWARE	NORTH CAROLINA
FLORIDA	NORTH DAKOTA
GEORGIA	OHIO
HAWAII	OKLAHOMA
IDAHO	OREGON
ILLINOIS	PENNSYLVANIA
INDIANA	RHODE ISLAND
IOWA	SOUTH CAROLINA
KANSAS	SOUTH DAKOTA
KENTUCKY	TENNESSEE
LOUISIANA	TEXAS
MAINE	UTAH
MARYLAND	VERMONT
MASSACHUSETTS	VIRGINIA
MICHIGAN	WASHINGTON
MINNESOTA	WEST VIRGINIA
MISSISSIPPI	WISCONSIN
MISSOURI	WYOMING

House Hunt

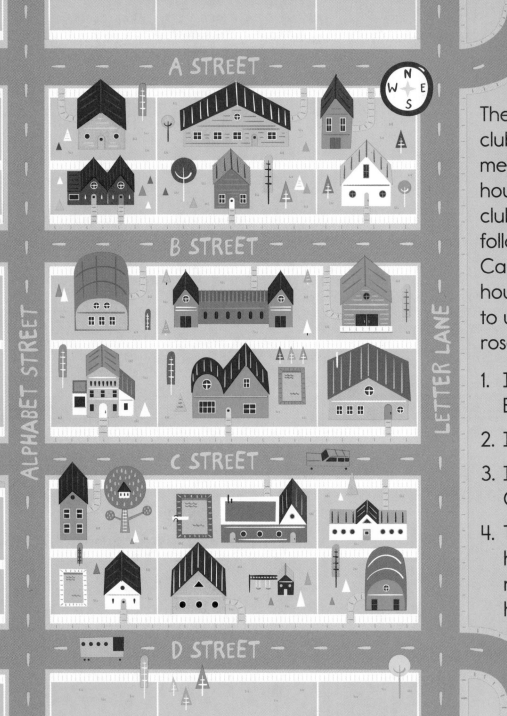

The geography club is having its first meeting at Marco's house. He gave the club members the following directions. Can you find his house? Remember to use the compass rose to help you.

1. I am south of B Street.

2. I live on a corner.

3. I am north of C Street.

4. There is a blue house directly north of my house.

BONUS!

When Marco's friend Zheng heads home from Marco's house, he travels 2 houses east, 2 houses north, and 1 house west. Which house is Zheng's?

Compass Code

To answer the riddle below, start at the North (N) circle. Then move in the directions listed and write the letters you find in the correct spaces. We did the first one to get you started.

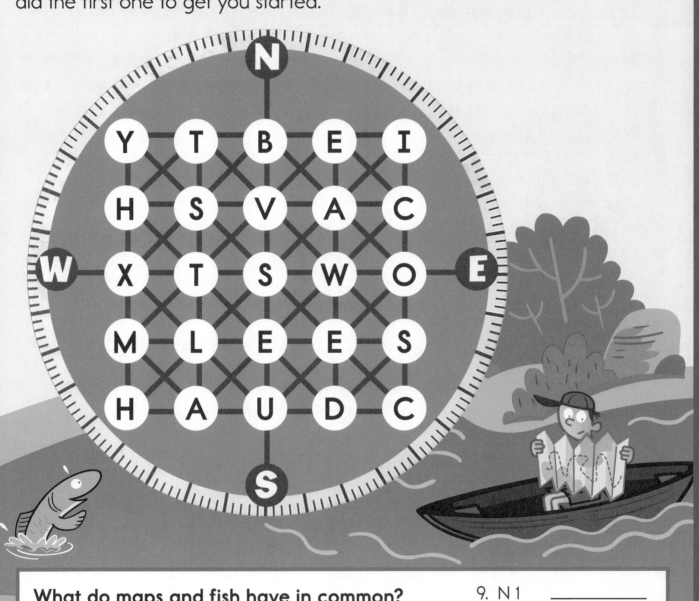

What do maps and fish have in common?

1. S 1 _____B_____

2. SE 2 _____

3. W 3 _____

4. NW 1 _____

5. S 3 _____

6. NE 3 _____

7. W 1 _____

8. S 2 _____

9. N 1 _____

10. SE 2 _____

11. W 3 _____

12. N 1 _____

13. E 2 _____

14. NW 2 _____

Weather Words

Use the clues to fill in the answers in this crossword puzzle.

ACROSS

1. Ice crystals on your window
2. Opposite of cold
5. Almost hot
7. Flash in the sky during a rainstorm
9. Icy "stones" that fall from the sky
10. Bright daylight
12. Slippery condition (rhymes with *spicy*)
14. Opposite of high
15. A blizzard or thundershower
16. Damp, muggy
17. What water will do below 32 degrees Fahrenheit
18. Very breezy

DOWN

1. Thick mist that's hard to see through
3. What thermometers measure
4. White, fluffy things in the sky
6. "Save it for a _____ day."
8. Loud "clap" in a rainstorm
11. Opposite of low
13. Opposite of hot
15. White flakes from the sky

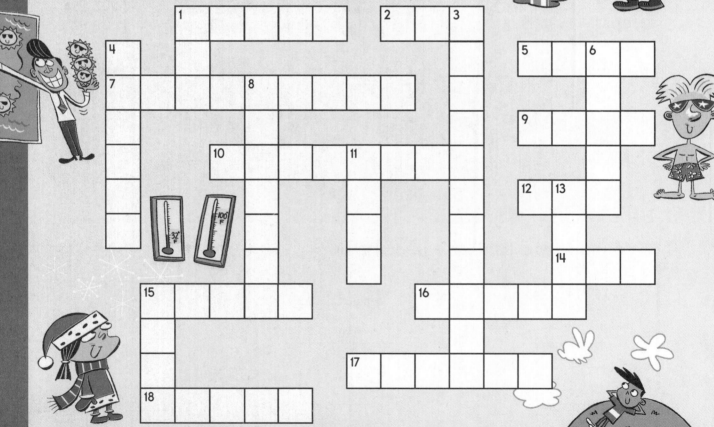

Liquid, Solid, and Gas

Water can be a liquid. Can you find drinking water in these pictures?
Water can be a solid. Can you find snow in these pictures?
Water can be a gas. Can you find steam in these pictures?

Can you find at least 10 differences between these scenes?

The Water Cycle

This picture shows Earth's water cycle. Read the definition for each part of the water cycle. Then color the arrows to show which part is which.

Find and circle **16** objects in this Hidden Pictures® puzzle.

Precipitation: Water falls from the clouds as rain or snow. Color the arrow that shows **precipitation** blue.

Evaporation: Water is heated by the sun and becomes part of the air in the form of water vapor. Color the arrow that shows **evaporation** orange.

Condensation: Water vapor cools as it rises and forms into clouds. Color the arrow that shows **condensation** green.

candy cane

broccoli

book

button

drumstick

piece of popcorn

celery

caterpillar

necklace

carrot

pinecone

grapes

heart

dog bone

crescent moon

balloon

Answers

Pages 4–5
Alphabet Maze

Pages 16–17
Bake Sale

Page 19
Prairie Dog Days

Page 22
I Like Knights

Page 24
Clues to Chew On

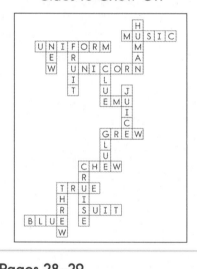

Pages 26–27
Snail Mail

Pages 28–29
Farm Party

Here are some *r*-controlled vowel words we found.
You might have found others.

acorn	horn
airplane	horse
barn	jar
bird	ladder
caterpillar	scarf
corn	skirt
feather	spider
flower	squirrel
fork	star
guitar	stork
hammer	turkey
heart	turtle

Page 30
Which Pair to Wear?

Page 31
Near the Pier

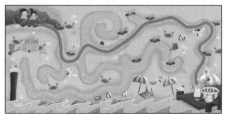

Page 32
What I Saw at Dawn

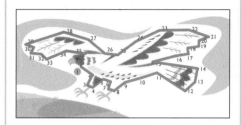

A HAWK

Page 33
Let's All Walk

THERE ARE 8 BEACH BALLS.

Pages 36–37
Chef Steve's Blends

Chef Steve only makes foods whose names start with a blend or digraph. Here are the words we made. You might have made others.

fly	chip	chat	chin	blab
cry	drip	flat	grin	crab
dry	flip	slat	shin	drab
try	ship	that	spin	grab
why	trip	what	thin	slab

blade	brim	blink	flare
grade	grim	clink	share
shade	slim	drink	snare
spade	trim	stink	spare
trade	whim	think	stare

Page 39
Spring Training

Page 41
Camp SiGHt Fright

Page 44
Words from Words

1. BAT
2. TEA
3. ASK
4. BELL
5. TALL
6. SALT
7. BAKE
8. LATE
9. BEST
10. LAKE
11. EAST
12. SKATE
13. LEAST
14. STABLE
15. BALLET

Page 45
Word Ladder

BIRD

1. BIND
2. BAND
3. WAND
4. WANT
5. WART
6. WARM

WORM

Pages 42–43
Shhhhhh!

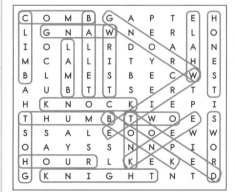

What is a librarian's favorite prehistoric creature?

A PTERODACTYL, BECAUSE THE P IS ALWAYS SILENT

Page 46
All Talk

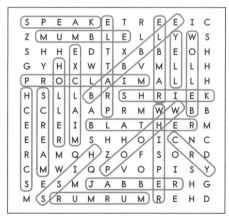

245

Answers

Page 47
Opposite Words

What goes up but never comes down?

YOUR AGE

Page 53
People, Places, Things

Page 59
Reflections

Page 60
Whose Smoothie?

Pages 48–49
Extraordinary

Pages 50–51
Time to Rhyme

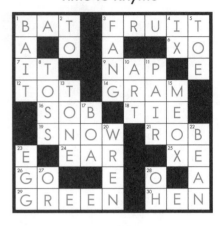

Pages 56–57
Where's My Sheep?

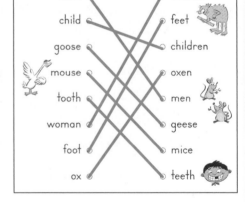

Pages 66–67
Splashing Around

Pages 68–69
It's a Maze!

Pages 70–71
A Fun Day

Pages 72–73
Comparing Animals

Page 74
Win or Lose

THERE ARE 16 HOCKEY STICKS.

Page 79
How? When? Where?

Page 80
Aa

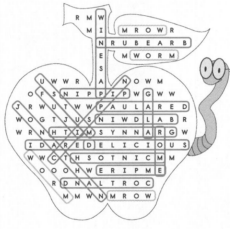

Page 81
Bb

Page 85
Ff

What did the bus driver say to the frog?
"HOP ON!"
Where do frogs take notes?
ON LILY PADS

Page 82
Cc

Page 83
Dd

THERE ARE 20 DINOSAURS.

Page 86
Gg

Answers

Page 88
Ii

```
D R A G O N F L Y X
C M O T H B I Z Q J
R B U T T E R F L Y
I X V Z W E E J T L
C Q G N A T F L E A
K A N T S L L O R D
E V Z J P E Y U M Y
T Z A P H I D S I B
H O N E Y B E E E T U
H O U S E F L Y E G
```

Page 89
Jj

Page 90
Kk

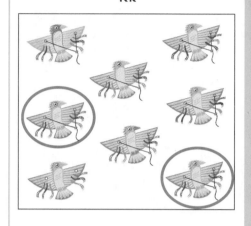

Page 91
Ll

Page 92
Mm

Page 94
Oo

```
        O C T A G O N
        W         V         O B O E
O V E R A L L S   E         N
        R     O R A N G E   E
        L     I         A
        I     O N I O N
        O V A L       C
        E             T
                      O
                      P
                      U
                      S
```

Page 95
Pp

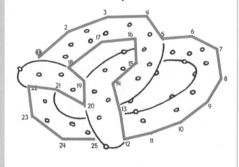

IT'S A PRETZEL.

Page 96
Qq

Page 97
Rr

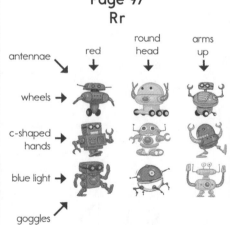

antennae   red   round head   arms up

wheels

c-shaped hands

blue light

goggles

Page 98
Ss

Page 99
Tt

Page 100
Uu

Here is one answer.
You may have found another.

Page 101
Vv

Page 102
Ww

SNOWMAN   SNOW CONE
SNOWSHOES   SNOWBALL   SNOWMOBILE

Page 103
Xx

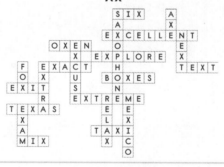

Page 104
Yy

Page 105
Zz

Pages 106–107
Storm Magic

1. raining.
2. disappointed
3. Katy
4. straw
5. out the window
6. The girls play on the swings.

Pages 108–109
Sun and Wind

1. Sun and Wind
2. He shivers and holds on to his hat.
3. When the sun smiles down on him
4. In the sky
5. Because he is warm
6. It smiles down on him.

Pages 110–111
Impossible to Train

1. dogs
2. They think the pets are impossible to train but love them anyway.
3. Sammy
4. Sammy
5. Because at first you think it is humans talking about dogs

Pages 112–113
Too Many Bags!

1. Rabbit's house
2. disorganized
3. helpful
4. He has too many bags.
5. He makes a jump rope out of the old bags by cutting off handles and braiding the strips together.

Answers

Pages 116–117
Warm Welcome

1. a boy
2. Welcome
3. shirt, bumblebees, by, guard
4. busy bumblebees/big backyard
5. excited/happy/welcoming

Pages 118–121
The King's Challenge

1. Middle
2. End
3. Beginning
4. Beginning
5. End
6. Overcome challenges

Pages 122–125
The Perfect Job for Odo

1. under each scene.
2. Odo.
3. Odo is tired of making kites.
4. Odo tries some new jobs.
5. He gets a job he likes taking care of babies.
6. They tell the story visually. (You may have come up with another answer.)

Pages 126–127
Butterflies in Disguise

1. an insect.
2. other butterflies.
3. hide from predators.
4. the ability to blend into the surrounding area

A3 B2 C1

Pages 128–129
Bubble Bonanza

1. "soft" or distilled water
   dish detergent
   glycerin or corn syrup
2. Put 3 cups of water in a bucket.
3. Let the mixture sit for a few hours.
4. 3
5. 2 straws
6. 6 times as long a a straw

Pages 130–131
Rubeosaurus/Tyrannotitan

Meat-eater
Plant-eater
40 feet long
12 feet long
Bones found in the United States
Bones found in South America
Horned
No horns
Babies hatch from eggs
Lived in herds
Lived alone
Lived in the Cretaceous period
Thick, strong back legs

Tyrannotitan

Both

Rubeosaurus

Pages 132–135
Chasing Chickens

1. Cheziya, Zimbabwe
2. Christmas
3. He whistles loudly.
4. Tinaye
   He follows it into the hut.
5. yearly
6. events
7. plan

Pages 136–137
Subway Subjects

Page 139
Carnival Objects

Which of these words can be both a verb and a noun?
RIDE   WIN

Page 141
Library Statements

Page 143
Bus-Stop Questions

Here is one answer.
You may have found another.

Page 144 Scrambled Exclamations

POP!	RING!	CHIRP!	SIZZLE!	GLUG!	BUZZ!
HONK!	POOF!	ACHOO!	OUCH!	GROWL!	PURR!

VROOM!

Page 147
Make a Pizza

Pages 148–149
Sorting Sentences

 STATEMENT

 COMMAND

I love my cat.

Feed my cat.

The flower is pretty.

Smell the flower.

 QUESTION

 EXCLAMATION

Where does this flower grow?

My cat is so beautiful!

What is my cat doing?

This flower is gigantic!

Page 151
Loose Lizard

Page 155
Thank You!

Page 162
A Comic Caper

Page 166
Two by Two

Page 167
Fun with Fives

There are 5 flowers, squirrels, birds, ants, clouds, and pieces of chalk.

Pages 170–171
Happy Hundredth!

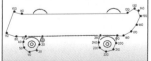

IT'S A SKATEBOARD.

251

Answers

Page 173
Purr-fect Numbers

Why are cats good at video games?
THEY ALL HAVE NINE LIVES.

Page 174–175
Amusing Numbers

Page 182
The Race Is On

Page 183
Number Flags

764 ○——○ seventy-six
245 ○——○ three hundred twenty-seven
536 ○——○ twenty-five
76 ○——○ two hundred forty-five
327 ○——○ three hundred sixty-three
25 ○——○ seven hundred sixty-four
363 ○——○ five hundred thirty-six

Pages 176–177
Pizza Fact Families

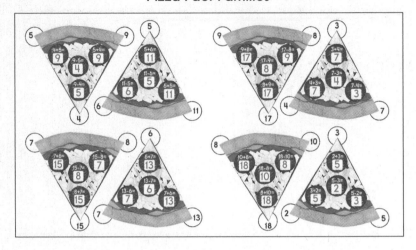

Pages 184–185
Sky High

Pages 186–187
Addition Mission

Pages 194–195
Turtle Crossing

24 + 48 = 72   28 + 13 = 41
39 + 15 = 54   21 + 46 = 67
56 + 27 = 83   29 + 27 = 56
33 + 11 = 44   52 + 15 = 67
24 + 13 = 37   72 + 9 = 81
72 + 11 = 83   83 + 12 = 95
41 + 21 = 62   60 + 23 = 83
39 + 28 = 67   28 + 16 = 44
52 + 47 = 99   47 + 34 = 81
59 + 19 = 78

What was the turtle doing
on the highway?

ABOUT ONE MILE PER HOUR!

Pages 196–197
Subtraction Action

Pages 198–199
What's the Difference?

Pages 204–205
The Art of Subtraction

GREEN PAINT

Pages 208–209
Score Big

The kangaroos are in the lead.

Page 216
Fraction Fun

What do you call three feet of trash?
A JUNKYARD

Who invented fractions?
HENRY THE EIGHTH

Pages 226–227
Time Codes

What do workers do in a clock factory?
MAKE FACES

When is a clock nervous?
WHEN IT'S ALL WOUND UP

Pages 220–221
Your Money's Worth . . .

$1.05   87¢   (\$1.41)

28¢   (96¢) $1.75

(\$1.38)   63¢ $1.23

94¢ $1.23   (85¢)

Angelo: NICKEL

Brett: PENNY

Ciara: NICKEL

Evan: DIME

Ahnah: QUARTER

Pages 228–229
Community Park

Answers

Page 230
Job Search

Page 235
Scrambled States

Light Blue: HAWAII

White: COLORADO

Red: IDAHO

Yellow: ALASKA

Green: NEVADA

Orange: KANSAS

Black: OREGON

Purple: ARIZONA

Dark Blue: UTAH

Pink: TEXAS

Pages 236–237
The Great State Search

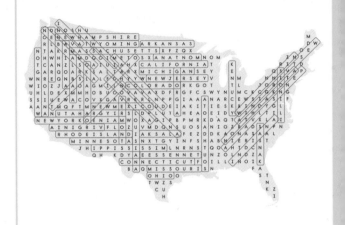

Page 238
House Hunt

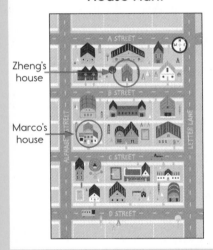

Page 239
Compass Code

BOTH HAVE SCALES

Page 240
Weather Words

Page 241
Liquid, Solid, and Gas

Pages 242–243
The Water Cycle

Page 256
Time for School!

254

Congratulations!

_____

(your name)

worked hard
and finished the

Second Grade
Big Fun Workbook

Time for School!

Find and circle **8** objects in this Hidden Pictures® puzzle. There are also **8** pencils hidden in this scene. Can you find them all?

hot dog

magnet

button

strawberry

penny

boomerang

key

seahorse